All Things Girl

Friends, Fashion, and Faith

Cheryl Dickow

The choicest first fruits of your soil
you shall bring to the house of the Lord,
your God.
~Exodus 23:19

References to the *Catechism of the Catholic Church* are denoted: *CCC*

Cover: Actiacti | Dreamstime.com
Interior Graphics: Izura Abdullah | Dreamstime; Rudall30 | Dreamstime; Nicky Linzey | Dreamstime; Gino Crescoli |Dreamstime; Frenta |Dreamstime; Madartists |Dreamstime; Aurelko |Dreamstime; Nikolaev |Dreamstime; Ivan Cholakov |Dreamstime; Carlos Caetano |Dreamstime; Lim Cheng En |Dreamstime; Milena Moiola |Dreamstime; Leong Kin Fei |Dreamstime; Jdgrant |Dreamstime; Mkoudis |Dreamstime

ISBN 978-1-936453-20-7

Table of Contents

You Are Here for a Reason

Your Sacred Beginning and Your Soul

All people begin life in their mother's womb. This is a sacred and special place. Mary carried Jesus in her womb. One day, if God is calling you to the vocation of marriage, you may carry a child in your womb. The person carried in the womb is made up of a body and a soul and is created in the image and likeness of God.

Every spiritual soul is created immediately by God. CCC#366

> ### *Your soul has important characteristics:*
> 1. It is immortal; it does not perish when it separates from the body at death.
> 2. It will be reunited with the body at the final resurrection.

Having a Soul Gives You Inherent Dignity...

Joan lives in a neighborhood where the houses are huge and everyone has a pool. Katie lives in a neighborhood where some of the houses have broken windows and lots of kids share bedrooms. Which person has more dignity?

Tamar is from the Middle East and has olive skin, she speaks with a thick accent. Mary has long, beautiful brunette hair and perfect skin. Betty is chubby and has greasy hair. Gertrude is skinny and cuts her own hair. Which girl has more dignity?

Olivia is 99 years old and can't bathe herself or feed herself. Ruby has a birthmark on the right side of her face. Jessica is a beautiful model who stars in television commercials. Which person has more dignity?

All people are equal in dignity because they've been given a soul by God at their creation.

Always remember that your soul is a precious gift from God!

A Sacramental Life

So you have a soul, right? That's what makes you special.

But it gets better. You see, when you are baptized, your soul is permanently marked and sealed by the Holy Spirit. It is a way in which you become a member of the body of Christ. Baptism is the first Sacrament and a lot of people call it the "door" to a spiritual life. Being baptized is part of living a Sacramental life. It washes away original sin and fills your soul with grace. It is the first step in answering  the big question "Why am I here?" You are baptized because you are here to know, love and serve God so that you can live happily with Him in eternity.

And living a Sacramental life helps you do just that.

Being baptized is really quite simple but its simplicity shouldn't make anyone underestimate its power! Have you ever noticed that during Easter Vigil the priest leads you through a renewal of your baptismal promises? That's because it is always good to remember what it means to be a baptized member of the body of Christ.

Check it out. This is an example of what the priest might say and what you would say in response.

- Do you reject Satan? I do.
  And all his works? I do.
  And all his empty promises? I do.
- Do you believe in God, the Father Almighty, creator of heaven and earth? I do.
- Do you believe in Jesus Christ, his only Son, our Lord, who was born of the Virgin Mary was crucified, died, and was buried, rose from the dead, and is now seated at the right hand of the Father? I do.
- Do you believe in the Holy Spirit, the holy Catholic Church, the communion of saints, the forgiveness of sins, the resurrection of the body, and life everlasting? I do.
- God, the all-powerful Father of our Lord Jesus Christ has given us a new birth by water and the Holy Spirit, and forgiven all our sins. May he also keep us faithful to our Lord Jesus Christ forever and ever. Amen.

Another part of living a Sacramental life is to take part in other Sacraments on a regular basis. By now you've probably had your First Holy Communion. Maybe there was a big party and maybe you had a very special dress that looked like a bride's dress. Or maybe you only had a couple of people watch as you received this Sacrament. No matter how big or how small the celebration was, receiving the Eucharist for the first time is a huge deal!

> ## This is because the bread and wine actually become the body and blood of Jesus. This is called Transubstantiation.

Baptism is a Sacrament that you receive only once in your life (even though you can continually renew the promises of it) while Communion is a Sacrament that you can receive over and over again, and should.

Going to Confession before receiving Communion can help you receive the body and blood of Christ in a state of grace. This is often called "receiving Communion worthily." Doing a daily Examination of Conscience also helps make sure that your heart is as clean as it can be for you to take in the body and blood of Jesus.

Here are some Examination of Conscience questions you might ask yourself at the end of your day, as part of your nightly prayer time:

1. **Did I remember to keep Jesus as part of my day today?**
2. **How did I treat my family members, friends and even strangers today?**
3. **Did I remember that every person has a soul and is a dignified person?**
4. **Did I do my chores or homework without complaining?**
5. **What did I do today that pleased God?**
6. **How did I show that I remember that I am a daughter of the King and my words and actions matter?**

Of course, these are only sample questions. You can make up your own—and should! The following pages are for your own Examination of Conscience questions. Share your answers with Jesus to make sure that He is always part of this special time and helps you keep a clean, honest, and loving heart.

Do You Live a Soulful Life?

Take this quiz to see if you are living a soulful life. These are Examination of Conscience questions that can help you see if you are living with the knowledge that you and every person you know is unique and dignified because of their soul. Circle your answer or record it someplace else. Make sure you are honest with yourself!

1) When something wonderful happens to a friend, like getting the best role in the school play, I am always happy for her—I am not jealous or envious because I know God has given her a soul and she is as loved as I am!
Sometimes   Always   Never

2) If a friend hurts me, I talk to her about it and forgive her without thinking of revenge or feeling sorry for myself because I know God has given her a soul and she is as loved as I am!
Sometimes   Always   Never

3) When someone makes fun of a friend—or even a stranger—I stand up for her because I know God has given her a soul and she is as loved as I am!
Sometimes   Always   Never

4) When I hurt someone, I apologize and then go to Confession because I know it is good for my soul.
Sometimes   Always   Never

5) When my mother asks me to do something, I honor her and do it without complaining because God gave me my mother for a reason and she gave me life—so that God could give me a soul!
Sometimes   Always   Never

Tally you answers and read the key below.

Mostly Never. You have a lot of work to do—but you probably already know that and God is giving you graces to grow in your spiritual life so that you can be all that He wants you to be!

Mostly Sometimes. You are living your life aware of the nature of your soul and the souls of those around you. Keep up the great work!

Mostly Always. You are a soulful person and doing a great job! Keep this up so that others can witness to how awesome it is to live this way!

Relationships

Friendships

Just as this quote suggests, a good friend knows a lot about you—what you like to do, who your family is, and what kinds of jokes make you laugh—and still loves you. Friends are wonderful to have. They give you great advice when you don't know what to do about a certain situation, they can listen to you as you tell them all about the awful day that you had, and—maybe more importantly, they are a lot of fun!

God does all things for a reason. This means that God made friends for a reason, too. Friends can help you study for a difficult test, give you advice on what dress to wear to a dance, or just plain hang out with you.

It's important to realize that you don't have to have a million friends in order to be happy. As long as you have a few trusted friends, you will be all set! Sometimes it can seem like you need to be friends with at least six or seven people, but this just isn't true. It is perfectly normal to have just two or three close friends, and some people even have just one good friend!

Have you ever heard of Saint Elizabeth Ann Seton?

She was born in 1774 in New York. Even though her family was part of the high society of New York, Elizabeth Ann Seton was often lonely. But this didn't stop her from becoming a great role model! She got married at the age of twenty, to a young man named William Seton.

Elizabeth and William loved each other greatly, but unfortunately, William's health started to get worse a couple of years into the marriage, so the couple had to move to Italy. When she and her husband were in Italy, Elizabeth impressed her friends with her kindness and sweetness. Her husband unfortunately died while she was in Italy, but she had her friends and her growing interest in the Catholic faith to help combat the sorrow. She converted to Roman Catholicism in 1805, and she and her friends worked together to open the first free Catholic school in America!

She also started a Sisterhood with her friends. When she died in 1821, she was a very holy woman, and she was also beloved by her friends. She became a saint in September of 1975. Saint Elizabeth Ann Seton may have started out being lonely, but that didn't last long. She was able to make friends, convert to Catholicism, start a free school in America, and start a Sisterhood to honor and praise God! That's pretty impressive!

So, even if you don't feel like the most popular girl in the world—it's okay! Being popular at school is all right, but it isn't the most important thing. If you have just a few tried and trusted friends, you'll be able to get through tough days, fights that you get into with your siblings, an illness in the family, or any other bad things that come your way. Remember: your friends love you no matter what. They are there for you to talk to, to get advice from, to learn from, and to have fun with.

So, what kind of friends should you look for? The most important thing to look for in a friend is their caring heart. A true friend will always want the best for you. And a good friend will not be envious of you if your parents buy you a new iPod or you get the chance to go on a cruise to the Bahamas. They will be happy that you are happy! A good friend will also help you through tough times. They will not leave you to deal with your parents' fight on your own—they will be right there, taking you out to see a movie to distract you, or bringing you your favorite kind of chocolate. A good friend always helps make things better—never worse! She gives you ways to cope, offers a shoulder to cry on, and maybe helps you to understand the other side of the story.

Another important thing to look for in a friend is that they have the same values as you do. If a friend believes that stealing is okay, or a friend thinks that making fun of an unpopular girl in class is a good idea, then this is not a good sign. A friend with the same values as you will know that stealing is wrong and that being nice is super important. A friend with the same values as you will help you become a better person, too!

> Whether it develops between persons of the same or opposite sex, friendship represents a great good for all. It leads to spiritual communion. *CCC # 2347*

Here are some examples of good friends to have:

Caring Christy
Christy is the kind of friend who is always there for you. If you are having a bad day, she has a joke ready to cheer you up. If you are sick, she makes a "Get Well" card for you. If you are happy, she is happy for you, too. She asks you how you are doing, and if you tell her that you're having a tough day, she's always ready to offer you a hug.

Advisor Allison
Allison is the friend who you can always turn to for good advice. If you don't know what to do about a bad grade that you got on your last test, or an argument that you just got into, she'll be there to help you figure out what to

do. Allison is great at coming up with solutions to problems, and you would trust her with your life!

Joyous Jamie

Jamie is the type of friend who is always happy and upbeat. She can see the positive in almost every situation. She also loves to have fun. She plans lots of parties, and loves to organize bonfires, shopping trips to the mall, and ice cream outings. You know that there will never be a dull moment if Jamie is around!

Fashionable Felicia

Felicia is the friend that you go to when you need help with your wardrobe. If you are freaking out about what to wear to a school dance, don't worry! Felicia will be there for you. She will either come over to your house and dig through your closet, looking for a great outfit hidden somewhere, or she'll lend you some of her own clothes. She has a big heart and wants you to look your best!

Athletic Alicia

Alicia is the friend who is great at sports. Whether she plays tennis, runs track, or swims, she is always up for a challenge and loves adventure. She's a great friend to play with. She's always up for a game of basketball, volleyball, or softball, and she makes the game fun! Alicia is a great friend to have if you want to be healthy and stay physically active.

Prayerful Paige

Paige is a great kind of friend to have! If you are going through a tough time, she always promises to pray for you. She also has a great sense of humor, and is a lot of fun to be around! She truly cares about you, and she wants you to have a wonderful relationship with your other friends, your family, and God.

These are all great types of friends to have! However, it's important to realize that not all friends are going to be so nice to you. Sometimes a friendship can turn bad, especially if a friend doesn't have the same values as you.

John Bosco, an Italian saint, once said:

Fly from bad companions as from the bite of a poisonous snake. If you keep good companions, I can assure you that you will one day rejoice with the blessed in Heaven; whereas if you keep with those who are bad, you will become bad yourself, and you will be in danger of losing your soul.

Like Saint John Bosco mentions, sometimes having bad friends is similar to the bite of a poisonous snake. If you aren't careful, they may be dangerous and harm you one day. That is why it is best to surround yourself with friends who are good, and who have the same values as you. But sometimes it isn't so easy to tell whether a friend is good or bad for you.

So, how do you tell if a friendship is healthy or not? If a friend ever lies to you, is mean to you, or talks about you behind your back, this is not a good sign for the friendship. That is not to say that you can't be friends with people who occasionally lie or gossip or act mean. Everyone is human, and everyone makes mistakes. God asks us to forgive the people in our life who have hurt us and who are truly sorry for what they have done. So, it isn't a bad thing to give somebody a second chance if they lie to you, are mean to you, or gossip about you. But a sign of trouble is when that "friend" does these things repeatedly to you. These are some types of so-called "friends" that you should possibly avoid:

- Friends who lie to you often or who pressure you into doing things that you are not comfortable with.
- Friends who are there for you when times are good, but leave you to figure things out on your own when times get bad.
- Friends who are boy-crazy, or who encourage you to chase after boys. That isn't healthy!
- Friends who talk about others behind their backs. They may seem nice to you, but if they are capable of being mean to others, they might get into a fight with you and treat you the same way they treat other girls.
- Friends who are never happy for you when good things happen to you or friends that easily get jealous of you.
- Friends who want all of the attention on them, and don't ever have time to listen to what you have to say.
- Friends who tell all of your secrets to everyone in school.
- Friends who are always negative and depressed.

As stated before, it is important to give friends second—and even third—chances. But when your friends repeatedly act in any of the ways listed above, it is important for your happiness to protect yourself from getting hurt. You love yourself, right? And when you love something, you want to protect it. So it follows that you have to protect yourself from friends who hurt you repeatedly.

If a friend is causing you trouble often—whether she is lying to you, encouraging you to chase after boys, or pressuring you into doing things that you aren't comfortable with—you can talk to your parents, teachers, or school counselors about the problem. Or, if you think that is too extreme, you can always be polite and kind to them when you see them at school or at the mall, while keeping your secrets and most private feelings safe from them.

Sometimes you can solve problems with your friends by just talking to them. If you talk to a friend about a problem that you are having with them, and they change the way that they treat you, then that's great! But if you talk to a friend about the way they are treating you, and they blow you off, then that isn't such a great sign. If that's the case, then you might want to consider either talking the problem through with your parents or a trusted adult, or trying the polite-but-distant approach with the friend.

It is true that friendships can be a challenge, but remember that God is always on your side. When you are having trouble with friends, you can bring your troubles to Him in prayer, as well. You can also always bring the good things about your friendships to prayer—you can thank God for the good times that you have with your friends, too.

God created man in his image and established him in his friendship.
CCC #396

Boys

It is okay—even great!—to be friends with boys. Boys are different from girls in many ways, and it is good to have a balance of friendships with both girls and boys. But if you're getting to the stage when you think that boys are cute, you might want to stop and think about what dating is all about.

Dating is all about trying to figure out if you and your boyfriend could be called to marriage. You are nowhere near marriage yet, are you? Then that probably means that you are not ready to date yet, either. Dating also involves a lot of decisions. Sometimes boys, especially as they are going through puberty, are really interested in being physically involved with girls. They may even pressure girls to make decisions that they are not comfortable with—like to kiss them when they are not ready. You can avoid the stress—and the devastation—that some girls experience when they start dating too soon by simply deciding not to date for now. This is the best choice that you can make! Since you are not ready to get married, you are not really ready to start dating yet, either.

It may be hard to make this decision and to stick with it, but once you do, it will make your life much simpler. You may have friends that are starting to date, and it may occasionally make you feel lonely. But the truth is that relationships at your age don't tend to last very long, and that girls who date before they are ready—or before parents say it is okay—too often end up getting hurt when those relationships don't end up turning out well. The best way to protect yourself from getting hurt is to stay away from dating—certainly for the time being. You also protect yourself by respecting what your parents have to say about all this; after all, they love you very much and always want the best for you! They won't steer you wrong—even if you don't agree with them, it is important to honor and respect their authority just as the 4th commandment instructs.

If you ever do feel lonely, just remember that you have friends, siblings, and family members to keep you company for now. And one day—when you are closer to being ready for marriage—you will be able to date and have that much more meaningful of a relationship because you didn't date frequently at the age that you're at now.

But despite the fact that you should hold off on dating for a while, you can still be friends with guys. Boys can be great friends. They are funny, interesting, and exciting to hang out with. As long as you hang out with guys in a group, you won't go wrong. It's perfectly fine to go bowling or to the mall with boys, just as long as you are in a group, and your mom or dad has given permission.

It is important that you don't try to change yourself for boys. Sometimes, a girl will think that a guy is cute, and suddenly decide that she doesn't like ballet anymore, just because the guy isn't interested in it. Or sometimes a girl will suddenly decide to pretend that she loves snowboarding just because a guy that she likes is really into it.

But God made you the way He did for a reason. You have special talents and gifts as a child of God. You may be an amazing clarinet player! Or you may love horses and dream of starting a horse farm one day. Maybe you are a top-notch softball player! Maybe you like pop music; or country; or classic rock. But whatever it is that you are talented at and like, don't ever give it up for a boy that you think is cute.

Boys that you think are cute will come and go out of your life, but one thing should always stay the same: who you are! Many girls try to change in order to please the guy that they have a crush on, but this never works out well. Think about it: would you be happy to find out that the friend you always thought loved horseback riding as much as you do actually just pretended to like it? No! You would be much happier if she just told you straight out that she loves swimming. Then you could learn about her hobby and discover something new that you like to do, too. The same thing is true with boys. They don't want to get to know someone you are only pretending to be. You are a cool girl, and if you act just like yourself, boys will want to be friends with you!

This still does not mean that you should date, but it is important and useful for you to have healthy friendships with boys. Boys often view things differently than girls, and find different things interesting, so their new perspective on things can definitely broaden a girl's view of the world!

The virtue of chastity blossoms in friendship.
It shows the disciple how to follow and imitate him who has chosen us as his friends,
who has given himself totally to us and allows us to participate in his divine estate.
Chastity is a promise of immortality.
CCC #2347

What Kind of Friend Are You?

Take this quiz to discover what kind of friend you are!

It's summer! It's a Saturday afternoon, and you and your friends are all hanging out in your bedroom. What would you suggest to do next?

A. Nothing. You like just hanging out and talking to your friends.
B. Go to the library to check out some good books or to browse the DVD section.
C. Go out for ice cream or go to the beach. Anything fun and relaxing!
D. Go swimming at the community pool, or start up a softball game in the backyard.
E. Go to the mall! You and your friends love shopping, especially for new clothes.

Your best friend calls you. She's really upset because she has just found out that she has to move out of the state. How would you try to comfort her?

A. Tell her that you're coming over to talk things over. Bring a box of Kleenexes and her favorite cookies along as cheering-up kit. You listen to all she has to say, offer her a hug, and promise to pray for her.
B. Look up some cool facts about the new place that she's moving to, and tell her all about them. That way she will be able to start getting excited about all of the new experiences that she will have!
C. Promise to spend all of your available time hanging out with her before she moves, and plan lots of fun activities for the two of you to do together before she moves, including a surprise good-bye party!
D. Offer to go on a walk or a run with her, so she can talk things out. The physical exercise won't be bad for her, either! A combination of exercise and talking will help reduce her stress.
E. Tell her how sorry you are that she's moving away, and offer to go to the mall with her. She'll need warmer clothes in Alaska! Plus, you just know that shopping will take her mind off of things.

Your teacher introduces a new girl to your class. She seems like she is nice and funny, and you want to become friends with her. How do you approach her?

A. You ask her a lot of questions about where she came from, what her interests are, and what she likes to do for fun.
B. You notice that she struggles with social studies. You're really good at social studies, so you offer to help her with her homework sometime.
C. You mention that you and your friends are having a pool party, and that she's welcome to come. The more the merrier!
D. You notice that her t-shirt has a picture of a basketball net on it, so you ask her if she plays basketball. Maybe she will be a new teammate!
E. You compliment her on her cute outfit, and ask her what her favorite clothing store is.

It's wintertime! You and your friends want to do something fun together, but you're not sure what. What do you suggest?

A. Stay inside next to the fire and drink hot cocoa, playing board games and hanging out with your friends.
B. Plan to learn something new, like how to make friendship bracelets, or how to make hard candy.
C. You have tons of ideas! You could go out to the movies, or play on the Wii, or have a snowball fight, or bake cookies. As long as it's fun, you're up for it!
D. Go outside and do something active, like sledding or ice skating!
E. Paint your fingernails! It is too cold to do anything outside, and this is the perfect opportunity to try out the new glow-in-the-dark fingernail polish that your cousin just bought you.

You and your best friend haven't talked to each other in a while. When you catch up with each other, what do you talk about?

A. All of the experiences that you've both had while separated, and how she feels about her grandma moving in with her family.
B. The great book that you've both just read.
C. All of the fun activities that you will do together, just as soon as school gets out for the summer.
D. How your sport game went, as well as how her dance recital went.
E. You devour your new issue of your fashion magazine together, and plan out what outfits you would both put together if you could.

Now, see which letter (A through E) that you chose the most often. Then find the matching description, and find out what kind of friend you really are!

A. The Supportive Friend

You are the friend that people go to when they need to talk about important issues. You are the kind of friend who is always willing to lend a listening ear to a friend in need. When a friend is having a bad day, you are right there with a box of chocolate to cheer her up. When a friend calls you in the middle of the night because she is worried about her band concert or her dance recital, you pick up every time. You are a great friend! You are able to help your friends cope with their emotions and feelings, and you are a wonderful listener. Your friends value you for your caring heart, your ability to listen well, and your sincerity.

B. The Smart Friend

You are the friend that people go to when they are looking for answers! You enjoy reading and learning, and you are always able (and willing) to help your friends with their schoolwork! If someone comes to you with a question about math or about English, you are able to help them work through the problem. You love learning new things and helping your friends learn new things, too! Your friends are important to you, and you show them that by helping them with their homework, learning new skills together, or discussing favorite books with them. Your friends value you for your curiosity, your intelligence, and your enthusiasm for learning new things!

C. The Fun-Loving Friend

You are the friend that people go to when they are looking to have a good time! You always have good ideas about what to do when everyone is sitting around, bored. Whether you suggest a trip to the beach, organizing a sleepover, or going out for ice cream, your friends are always inspired by your ability to find fun things to do! Your friends value your sense of humor, your upbeat attitude, and your creativity when it comes to finding fun things to do! You are a wonderful kind of friend to have around.

D. The Athletic Friend

You are the friend that people go to when they are looking for a fun game. You are awesome at playing sports! You are up to the challenge of playing whatever kind of game somebody wants to play. When you and your friends are sitting around, bored, you are the first to suggest a good game of volleyball or soccer. You love your friends, and you want them to be happy, physically active, and healthy. You show your love of your friends through playing sports or other games with them! Your friends value you for your high-energy level, your optimism, and your enthusiasm.

E. The Fashion Advisor

You are the friend that people go to when they are looking for advice on clothes, music, or the latest technology. When it comes to the latest styles and trends, you are on top of things. You know what looks good on your friends, and what doesn't—and, what's even better—you are willing to tell your friends the truth about their fashion choices! You love putting together unique and awesome outfits, and your friends love that you help them, too! They often come to you, either to ask for advice on what to wear to a dance, or to borrow your clothes. You care deeply about your friends and you show your love for them through your fashion advice! Your friends value your ability to be up-to-date, your creativity, and your eye for good style.

The Colors of Friendship

Did you know that colors represent different characteristics? Well, they do! The next time you and a friend are looking for something to do, consider going to an arts and crafts store and gathering some colored beads and other supplies to make a friendship bracelet or necklace; or maybe you can make a beautiful poster with a Scripture verse on it and use different colors. Here's what some different colors indicate:

Yellow
Yellow represents joy. True joy comes from knowing God loves you. Joy that comes from knowing God's love is a joy that you will always have, no matter what your circumstances. No one can take joy away from you.

Blue
Blue represents loyalty. Being loyal to Jesus is important. You become loyal by learning about Him and spending time with Him in prayer and in sharing your day. Jesus is completely loyal to you which is why He died for you.

Green
Green represents forgiveness. Forgiveness is an important trait to practice. It helps to remember that Jesus forgave your sins and so you should forgive others for the pains or hurts they may cause you; but remember that forgiving someone doesn't mean you have to be friends with someone who is always mean to you. If necessary, re-read the section on Relationships.

Orange
Orange represents compassion. Compassion is feeling love and concern for someone. Compassion can motivate people to do great things. Consider what Mother Teresa did for others because of her compassion. If you don't know about her, check out a book on Mother Teresa and really learn what compassion is all about!

Pink
Pink represents kindness. When you are kind to someone you show you care by sharing their joy and being loyal to them. Sometimes God will give you opportunities to be kind to people who aren't kind to you. Don't miss out on those opportunities because those are the times that you show your loyalty to God—which is the best loyalty to have

Red
Red represents love. Love often seems like a feeling but really it is a very big decision to be committed to someone, even if you don't "feel" very loving. You may not always feel loving towards your siblings but you should always be committed to caring for them and watching out for them. That is true love.

Purple
Purple represents royalty. You are royalty because you are a member of God's family. Everything you do and say should show that you understand your royal inheritance—that means in a humble way and never bossy or boisterous (loud)—and never, ever in a braggy, obnoxious way! Royalty is practicing kindness, love, and compassion.

White
White represents purity. God sees the pureness of our hearts and asks that we try to see each other that way as well. Not always easy, but something we are supposed to try to do.

Jesus wants to be your very best friend! Will you let him? Write a note to Jesus inviting him into a special friendship with you:

The Real You

The Real You

"Spread love everywhere you go: first of all in your own house. Give love to your children, to your wife or husband, to a next door neighbor... Let no one ever come to you without leaving better and happier. Be the living expression of God's kindness; kindness in your face, kindness in your eyes, kindness in your smile, kindness in your warm greeting."
~Blessed Mother Teresa of Calcutta

You know that loving others is super important, right? Just like Blessed Mother Teresa has said, showing your love to other people doesn't have to be hard. You can start with the people closest to you, including your mom and dad, your siblings, and your friends. Sometimes showing love to people can be as simple as smiling at them, holding a door open for them, or giving them a hug when they are feeling sad. Whenever you do something to help someone else out, you are showing them love! That means that when you clean your room without complaining, or help your younger sister with her homework, you are really practicing love.

Right now, it may seem pretty easy to show your love to others. Your job is to love and respect your parents, to learn new things at school, to be a good friend, and, if you have siblings, to be a great sister and role model. But what about when you grow up? How do you know what you're being called to do as an adult? How will you show your love to God (and people!) when you get to be 20, or 30, or 40? Will you get married and start a family, or will you live a single life and spend your weekends volunteering at the Church? Will you join a religious order and become a sister or a nun? Believe it or not, these are the kinds of questions that people ask when they are trying to figure out what their vocation is!

Has anyone ever asked you what you think your vocation might be? It may have seemed like a complicated question at the time, but it's really a lot simpler than you think! That person was really asking you: Do you know what God is calling you to do with your life? That's all! So, a *vocation* is a calling from God. God loves us so much that He has a plan for everyone. That's pretty awesome when you stop to think about it. When you try to figure out what God's plan is for you, you are *discerning your vocation*. Or, in other words, you are trying to figure out what God is calling you to do for the rest of your life!

So, who has a vocation? Is it just people who eventually become priests or nuns? Not at all! Every Christian has a vocation. When you were baptized as an itty-bitty, teeny-tiny baby, you were called to know, love, and serve God throughout your life. This call—to know, love, and serve God—is one part of having a vocation!

Another part of having a vocation deals with your own, personal relationship with Jesus. As a Christian, you are called to have a great relationship with Jesus Christ. You are meant to talk to Him in prayer, to learn about Him from the Bible, catechism class, and going to Mass, and to love and serve Him by loving and serving others! When you try to be as close to Christ as possible, then you are really living out your vocation (call from God).

Finally, trying to discern your vocation (figure out your calling) involves asking God to help you understand what *state* in life He wants you to be in. This is where the priests and nuns come in! There are three states in life that God calls people to:

- The Consecrated Life
- The Married Life
- The Single Life

In other words, God may be calling you to join a religious community and become a sister or a nun (the consecrated life), to get married and be open to the possibility of having children (the married life), or to stay single and use your gifts to help the Church and serve other people (the single life).

The Consecrated Life

You may be called to the consecrated life! Women who are called to the consecrated life become either nuns or sisters. Nuns and sisters give up some things in the *secular* world (non-religious world), like their own houses and possessions. They share everything that they own with one another. Nuns and sisters are also supposed to live in community with one another, although in some cases, some sisters do live on their own. That means that if you become a nun or a sister, you won't be lonely. You will have very special relationships with the other nuns/sisters in your community.

Nuns are *cloistered*; that is, they live in a convent (a special building for the community of women) and do not have access to the public. That means that nuns only ever see each other, unless they get special permission from the Bishop. That doesn't mean that they are lonely, though! These nuns spend a lot of time in prayer, talking to God. They also have a very special relationship with each other, and strive to live in loving harmony. An example of an order that is cloistered is the Carmelite Order, which has been around for centuries! Carmelites have a special devotion to Mary, Jesus' mother. Nuns like Carmelites choose to spend their lives away from the rest of the world so that they can concentrate on prayer. That's pretty cool!

Sisters are not cloistered. That means that they are free to see and talk with the public. Sisters try to live out the Gospel by spending time in both prayer and by demonstrating acts of love. That means that sisters often open up schools, or do some sort of volunteer work for the poor. An example of an order that has sisters is the Franciscan Order. Sisters are important because they help teach about the faith, spend time praying, and really try hard to make the world a better place!

Women who are called to the consecrated life (whether as sisters or nuns!) take vows of poverty, chastity, and obedience to Christ. This means that they get rid of all of their personal possessions and share everything with one another. This also means that they promise to be pure and to follow Christ!

The Married Life

You may be called to the married life! Married life, just like the consecrated life and the single life, is a beautiful vocation. Women who are called to the married life participate in the Sacrament of Matrimony. They promise to love and cherish their husband for the rest of their life, in sickness and in health. The husband makes the same promises to the woman on the day of the marriage. That means that the wife and the husband are supposed to help take care of each other always, whether times are good or bad. That's pretty amazing!

When you get older, if you feel that you are being called to the Sacrament of Matrimony, you should pray about it. If God has a plan for you to be a wife, He will help you find someone to share the rest of your life with! If this is your vocation, keep in mind (for the future) that couples who have similar belief systems and pray together, often have much stronger, healthier relationships than those that don't.

Once married, couples are meant to love each other, serve God, and be open to the possibility of children. Sometimes God may have a plan for a married couple to have only one child, and sometimes God may have a plan for a married couple to have nine children! It all depends. Married couples don't always have children, either. Married couples who are unable to have children can serve God in different ways—they can help out at the local soup kitchen, volunteer at the elementary school, or plan Vacation Bible School for their church.

Couples who *do* have children, though, have certain responsibilities towards them! Parents are supposed to take care of their children - and this doesn't just mean feeding them and making sure that they go to school! Parents are also supposed to help their kids learn about their faith, teach them how to pray, and help them grow up to become good adults. If you are called to the married life, you will eventually be called to love your husband *and* your children.

Mary, Jesus' mother, is a good saint to pray to if you feel that you are called to the married life. Jesus' family is the most perfect family that you will ever see! Mary was sinless and a perfect mother. Joseph, her spouse, treated her with great love. He also protected her and Jesus from Herod's soldiers by fleeing to Egypt after being warned by a dream. And Jesus is the Messiah Himself! You couldn't find a more perfect family anywhere if you tried. Mary was a wife *and* a mother, so if you need advice about your possible call to marriage, she is the perfect saint to pray to!

The Single Life

Maybe you aren't called to either the married life or the consecrated life. What's a girl to do, then? Well, you're probably being called to the single life! The single life is another beautiful way of following God's call. You may think that the single life is only for girls who can't find someone to marry, or who don't want to join a religious order. That isn't true, though. Girls who are called to the single life find other ways to live out the love that Jesus taught us all about.

Girls who are called to the single life are often very involved in their parishes. They are often blessed with more time than married couples or sisters/nuns, and they put that time to good use! People who are called to the single life may teach religious education classes at their church, spend their free time helping out at nursing homes or soup kitchens, or organize Bible studies. The possibilities are endless!

The single life is not a lonely life. People who are called to the single life often form close relationships with people from church, fellow volunteers, and friends. People who are called to a single life also often have a career. Of course, you can have a career as a married woman, but it becomes more complicated when you have to balance your career and your family. If you are eventually called to the single life, you will be able to place more of your focus on your career. That could be a really great thing! For example, if you become a doctor, you might be able to help more people and dedicate more hours to your job than a married woman would be able to.

God created different vocations on purpose! Those who are called to the consecrated life are devoted to prayer and charity work. Those who are called to the married life are called to love their spouse and children, and try to help them make it to Heaven. Those who are called to the single life are called to use their careers and free time to help glorify God's name and to spread His love. That's pretty cool, isn't it?

How Do I Figure Out My Vocation?

So, whether you're called to the consecrated life, the married life, or the single life, God has beautiful plans in store for you. Yes, you! Right now, you are called to love your parents, friends, and siblings. You aren't ready to get married or join a religious order yet! So what can you do to get ready for a future vocation?

The answer is simple . . . you can pray! Ask God to help you figure out which vocation you will eventually be called to. Maybe you'll be lucky, and He will answer you quickly. Sometimes, though, it takes a while to really hear what God is telling you. It's a good idea to start asking God for help now, so you can be ready to hear His answer in the future!

Being a Girl Is So Awesome!

Have you ever thought about how cool it is that God made you into a girl? There are so many awesome things that girls get to do—have sleepovers, join a girl's club, or go on shopping trips, to name a few—and girls have pretty special personalities, too. God made you a girl for a reason. He even gave you special gifts as a girl! As a girl, you may be more:

- Wise
- Kind/Caring
- Empathetic (understanding other people's perspectives)
- Nurturing (taking care of, and encouraging, others)
- Social
- Loyal
- Faithful
- Generous
- Sincere

These are all really great gifts to have! Boys also have these gifts but often a girl has them more abundantly. God also gives special gifts to boys—you may have them as well, but boys tend to have them more abundantly than girls. Do you think He gave the same gifts to boys as He gave to girls? No! Of course not. Girls and boys are different in a lot of ways, and God knows that! So God gave girls special gifts to use *as girls*, and He gave boys special gifts to use *as boys*.

Now, how do you think you can use your gifts as a girl today? Maybe you could comfort a friend who is having a bad day by giving them a hug. Or maybe you could offer to babysit your little cousin! Or if you can't do either of these things, maybe you could just spend some extra time with your friends today, being social. Any of these things will help you practice using your gifts that God gave you!

God also gave girls tons of fun things to do. If you're ever bored, try one of these ideas to liven up your day!

- Ask for permission from your parents and bake something!
- Learn how to make a friendship bracelet.
- With help from your mom, plan a sleepover!
- Invite some friends over and learn how to paint your fingernails.
- Go on a shopping trip to the mall.
- Make your own journal.
- Make silly putty.
- Ask your mom to help you learn how to sew something.
- If your parents have a video camera and will let you and your friends use it, make a movie with your friends!
- Tell a story - get some friends together, and have everyone sit in a circle. Have the first person in the circle tell the first 2-3 sentences of the story, and then move onto the next person!
- Play a game of kickball or dodge ball.
- Put on a puppet show—for your friends or for your younger siblings.

Recipe for Chocolate Oatmeal Chocolate Chip Cookies

1 ¼ c. margarine
1 c. sugar
1 t. vanilla
1 egg
1 c. flour
½ t. baking soda
½ t. salt
6 T. cocoa powder
¼ c. water
3 c. oats
1 c. chocolate chips

Key
c. = cup
t. = teaspoon
T. = tablespoon

Directions: In a mixing bowl, cream **margarine** and **sugar**. Next, add the next eight ingredients (everything except the chocolate chips). Mix well. Gently fold in chocolate chips. Drop, by teaspoonfuls, onto a cookie sheet. Bake at 350° for 10-12 minutes. Remove cookie sheet and place cookies on a cooling rack. Once cool, serve and enjoy!

How to Make Silly Putty

Elmer's white glue
1 T. Borax (a powdered soap found in grocery stores)
1 c. water
Food coloring
Empty plastic pop bottle with lid
Zip-lock bag (quart-size)

Directions:

1. Mix the **Borax** with the **water** (1 cup). Stir until almost all of the powder dissolves. This is your **Borax mixture.**
2. Put 1 tablespoon of **Elmer's white glue** into your **zip-lock bag.** Add 1 teaspoon of water. Mix together.
3. If you want, you can make your silly putty colorful by adding one drop of **food coloring.**
4. Add 1 tablespoon of your **Borax mixture** to the bag of glue and water. You may have some extra **Borax mixture** when you've finished - you can either label it and store it in your empty plastic pop bottle or you can get rid of it.
5. Seal the bag tightly. Squish together for about 2 minutes with your fingers. When the mixture starts feeling like putty, then you can remove it from the bag and use it to play with!
6. When you're done making the silly putty, make sure to wash your hands well and help clean up. Enjoy!

There are so many cool things to do as a girl! You can probably come up with your own ideas of things to do, too. If you can, write down your list of things to do. Then you can pull it out the next time that you're bored.

You're so lucky to be a girl!

There's so many awesome things that you get to do. You get to have a pretty great personality, too. God sure knew what He was doing when He made girls, didn't He?

Write down some of the things that *you* love about being a girl here:

The Real You Quiz

Have you ever wondered what your own brand of "feminine genius" is? Which feminine gift did God bless you with? Take this quiz to find out!

Circle the answer that best describes you.

The Blue Section

1. When somebody makes fun of one of my friends, I stick up for her.
   Almost Always (4 pts.)   *Sometimes* (2 pts.)   *Almost Never* (0 pts.)
2. Even if the rest of my classmates are angry at a friend of mine, I still eat lunch with her in the cafeteria and play with her at recess.
   Almost Always (4 pts.)   *Sometimes* (2 pts.)   *Almost Never* (0 pts.)
3. When a friend of mine gets sick, I go visit her.
   Almost Always (4 pts.)   *Sometimes* (2 pts.)   *Almost Never* (0 pts.)
4. When a friend needs support for a sports game or a try-out for a school play, I am there cheering her on!
   Almost Always (4 pts.)   *Sometimes* (2 pts.)   *Almost Never* (0 pts.)

The Pink Section

1. When a friend of mine needs advice, they come to me.
   Almost Always (4 pts.)   *Sometimes* (2 pts.)   *Almost Never* (0 pts.)
2. When it looks like it is about to rain, I bring an umbrella or a raincoat.
   Almost Always (4 pts.)   *Sometimes* (2 pts.)   *Almost Never* (0 pts.)
3. When I make a decision, I think about what the consequences will be.
   Almost Always (4 pts.)   *Sometimes* (2 pts.)   *Almost Never* (0 pts.)
4. When one of my friends is about to make a bad decision, I tell her why I don't think she should do it.
   Almost Always (4 pts.)   *Sometimes* (2 pts.)   *Almost Never* (0 pts.)

The Orange Section

1. When a friend is having a bad day, I offer her a hug or try to cheer her up.
   Almost Always (4 pts.)   *Sometimes* (2 pts.)   *Almost Never* (0 pts.)
2. When I notice that somebody has too many bags to open a door on their own, I open it for them.
   Almost Always (4 pts.)   *Sometimes* (2 pts.)   *Almost Never* (0 pts.)
3. When I see that my little brother or sister is having a hard time doing his/her homework, I offer to help him/her with it.
   Almost Always (4 pts.)   *Sometimes* (2 pts.)   *Almost Never* (0 pts.)
4. When I see someone who looks lonely, I smile at them and say hello.
   Almost Always (4 pts.)   *Sometimes* (2 pts.)   *Almost Never* (0 pts.)

The Purple Section

1. When my mom bakes extra cookies for me to bring to school, I share them with everybody.
   Almost Always (4 pts.)   *Sometimes* (2 pts.)   *Almost Never* (0 pts.)
2. When a friend gets a cool gift for Christmas or gets to go on vacation, I am really happy for her.
   Almost Always (4 pts.)   *Sometimes* (2 pts.)   *Almost Never* (0 pts.)
3. When I get a new game to play on the Wii or on the computer, I let my brothers and sisters play with it, too.
   Almost Always (4 pts.)   *Sometimes* (2 pts.)   *Almost Never* (0 pts.)
4. When I have extra change in my pocket, I give it to people who are collecting donations for charities.
   Almost Always (4 pts.)   *Sometimes* (2 pts.)   *Almost Never* (0 pts.)

Great! Now that you've answered the questions, add up how many points you got in each section. The section that you've gotten the most points in describes you the best! And, if you want, you can figure out your second strongest feminine gift, as well! And, you can also consider ways to improve where your weaker "self" is so that you can serve God more fully as you grow up and continue to unwrap your "feminine gifts."

The Blue Section - Loyalty
Congratulations! Your strongest feminine gift is . . . LOYALTY! You are a very loyal daughter, friend, and sister. When your friends need someone to stick up for them, you are always right there, ready to stand up for them. When your friends are nervous about doing well during a try-out, they can count on you to be there, backing them up. Loyalty is a very important feminine gift to have—and to share with others. In the Bible, Ruth from the Old Testament showed the virtue of loyalty by telling her mother-in-law, Naomi, that she would move to Bethlehem with her. Read more about her in the Book of Ruth!

The Pink Section - Wisdom
Congratulations! Your strongest feminine gift is . . . WISDOM! You are a very wise girl. Your friends often come to you for advice, because they know that you think things through and are very level-headed. You understand how the world works, and you know that every action you take has consequences, whether good or bad. Your friends really prize you for your common sense, your foresight, and your ability to make great decisions. In the Bible, Mary of Bethany (her sister was Martha) was a wise woman. While Jesus was visiting her and her sister, Martha, she sat and listened to Jesus. Martha got angry because Mary wasn't helping her work, but Jesus reminded Martha that Mary was doing the more important thing - spending time with Him! Read more about Mary of Bethany in the Gospels of Luke and John.

The Orange Section - Compassion
Congratulations! Your strongest feminine gift is . . . COMPASSION! You are very kind and caring. When your friends feel sad, you try to cheer them up. You look for things to do that can help people, and you love making someone else's day seem brighter by doing little things to make them smile. Your friends admire you for your big heart and your gift of really listening to what they have to say.

In the Bible, Dorcas (also known as Tabitha) had the feminine gift of compassion. She dedicated her life to helping people - she did many good works and acts of charity. When she died of an illness, many people mourned her death. The Apostle Peter eventually raised her from the dead through prayer to Jesus Christ. Read more about Dorcas in Acts.

The Purple Section - Generosity
Congratulations! Your strongest feminine gift is . . . GENEROSITY! You are an extremely generous girl. When you are given something - whether it is a new game, delicious baked goods, or a book—you are excited to share it with others. You have a big heart and want to see other people enjoy the same privileges that you do. You have discovered a really important secret about the world—that the best things in life are shared! Your friends admire you for your willingness to give, and your cheerful attitude. In the Bible, the unnamed widow who puts two bronze coins into the temple treasury displays the feminine gift of generosity. Even though those two coins were probably the only money the widow had, she was willing to give them up—now, *that* is generosity! Read more about the widow in the Gospel of Luke.

Now, take a couple of minutes and think about how you can use *your* special feminine gift(s) to help make the world a better place. Here's some space to write down your thoughts:

Here are a few excerpts from the 1995 *Letter to Women* by Pope John Paul II

Read each excerpt and spend time determining what it means to you. Consider sharing the excerpts with your mother or grandmother or aunt or good friend.

John Paul II's words are in pink;
An explanation follows and it is in purple;
The questions you can ask yourself about each statement are in black.

Before you begin, ask the Holy Spirit to guide your thinking and discussion. Consider journaling your answers or making Examination of Conscience questions from these excerpts to help you live the message of your soulful dignity.

"I would now like to *speak directly to every woman,* to reflect with her on the problems and the prospects of what it means to be a woman in our time. In particular I wish to consider the essential issue of the *dignity* and *rights* of women, as seen in the light of the word of God."

> Or, in other words, John Paul II is saying that he would like to talk to all women about the problems that they face today, as well as all of the things they have to look forward to. He especially wants to talk about two issues: the dignity (the self-worth that we are all born with!) and the rights of women. He wants to talk about these two issues by looking at them from the standpoint of the "word of God."

Questions you might ask yourself:
- Why was it important for JPII to "speak directly to every woman?"
- What do you think he was concerned with in regards to women's issues and what women (and that means you!) may think or feel about themselves?
- What does the world try to tell you about your dignity and rights?
- How does looking at yourself in the light of the word of God differ from looking at yourself in the light of the world's messages?

"This "dialogue" really needs to begin with a word of thanks."

> Or, in other words, JPII says that this talk needs to start by saying thank you to every girl.

Questions you might ask yourself:
- What does our faith teach us about gratitude?
- Can you find any particular Gospel messages about thanksgiving and appreciation?
- Do you find that you value and appreciate and show gratitude for the things in your life that deserve such acknowledgment?
- How does having an attitude of gratitude make you a more "soulful" person?

"Thank you, women who are mothers! You have sheltered human beings within yourselves in a unique experience of joy and travail."

> Or, in other words, JPII says thank you to all women who are mothers. Mothers who have had babies in their wombs have had a special experience of both joy and difficult/painful work.

Questions you might ask yourself:
- Motherhood is a vocation that many women are called to; have you begun asking God what your vocation will be?
- Do you recognize how your own mother responded to God's call to bring you into the world?
- What do you think are some of the joys and travails (difficulties) of motherhood?

"Thank you, women who are wives! You irrevocably join your future to that of your husbands, in a relationship of mutual giving, at the service of love and life."

> Or, in other words, JPII says thank you to all women who are wives. When women get married, they join their future to the future of their husbands. The relationship of marriage is a relationship of giving – the husband gives to the wife, and the wife gives to the husband. When you join your future with your husband's future, you are doing it for two good things – love and life.

Questions you might ask yourself:
- What is JPII saying about the Sacrament of Marriage?
- How should marriage represent the Trinity?
- Why is it important for a marriage to have Christ at its center?

"Thank you, women who are daughters and women who are sisters! Into the heart of the family, and then of all society, you bring the richness of your sensitivity, your intuitiveness, your generosity and fidelity."

> Or, in other words, JPII says thank you to women who are daughters and/or sisters. Daughters and sisters bring wonderful things into the heart of the family, and then into all of society. Among these wonderful gifts are your sensitivity (being aware of, and open to, the feelings of others), your intuitiveness (your ability to instinctively, or naturally, know something), your generosity (your willingness to share), and your fidelity (loyalty).

Questions you might ask yourself:
- What is JPII saying about the value of females in the family?
- What "gifts" do you have that you want to embrace and develop—gifts that are truly feminine?

- How does fidelity (commitment) to Christ and to the Church's teachings enhance your soulfulness?

"Sadly, very little of women's achievements in history can be registered by the science of history. But even though time may have buried the documentary evidence of those achievements, their beneficent influence can be felt as a force which has shaped the lives of successive generations, right up to our own."

> Or, in other words, John Paul II is saying that a lot of women's achievements haven't been written down (or even recognized) throughout history. This is a sad thing. But even though these achievements haven't been written down, they have still had a wonderful effect on society. The achievements of women have affected the generations before us and our own generation.

Questions you might ask yourself:
- What is JPII saying about the history of humanity and women's achievements?
- What do you think JPII wants you to know about being a female?
- How might JPII's words change your own attitude about embracing the gift that is you!

"Women will increasingly play a part in the solution of the serious problems of the future: leisure time, the quality of life, migration, social services, euthanasia, drugs, health care, the ecology, etc."

> Or, in other words, JPII says that women are going to play a big role in finding solutions to serious problems in the future. Some of the issues that they will deal with are: leisure time (free time), the quality of life, migration (the movement of one place to another), social services (services that help people), euthanasia (so-called "mercy" killing), drugs, health care, the ecology (the study of animals, plants, etc. and their environments), etc.

Questions you might ask yourself:
- According to JPII, how important will women's contributions be for the future of the entire world?
- How do you think you accomplish all that God has planned for you?
- What do you already see as your unique talents—which are gifts from God meant for His glory and His kingdom?

"Womanhood and manhood are complementary not only from the physical and psychological points of view, but also from the ontological."

> Or, in other words, John Paul II says that both women and men are complementary. Being complementary means a couple of different things. First of all, it means that men and women

complete each other. It also means that men and women are different, and have different gifts, but that when these gifts are joined together, they create a whole. So it is equally important for there to be women as it is for there to be men, and both need each other.

Questions you might ask yourself:
- Can you think of things that complement each other—that are meant to go together—and understand what JPII is saying when he writes that "womanhood and manhood are complementary?"
- Why is it important for things that are complementary to stay the way they were made and not try to be too much like each other?

"The Church sees in Mary the highest expression of the "feminine genius" and she finds in her a source of constant inspiration. Mary called herself the 'handmaid of the Lord' (Lk 1:38)."

> Or, in other words, John Paul II says that the Catholic Church believes that Mary is the greatest example of feminine genius (or, basically, that she is the best example of what being a girl is really about!). Mary, Jesus' mother, is inspirational to the Catholic Church. That means that the Catholic Church looks up to and admires her a lot. Mary called herself the "handmaid of the Lord". A handmaid is a female servant. So, Mary called herself a servant of the Lord.

Questions you might ask yourself:
- How is it possible to have "feminine genius"—which seems like something to really brag about!—and yet still be a "handmaid of the Lord"?
- Why is Mary an excellent role model for you?

"And how can we overlook the many women, inspired by faith, who were responsible for initiatives of extraordinary social importance, especially in serving the poorest of the poor? The life of the Church in the Third Millennium will certainly not be lacking in new and surprising manifestations of 'the feminine genius'."

> Or, in other words, JPII is saying that it is also important to remember the many women who did extremely important social work. These women were inspired by faith. These women especially helped serve the poorest people in the world. In the Third Millennium, there will be lots of new and surprising examples of women who show the "feminine genius" (use their God-given talents as women to change the world for the better).

Questions you might ask yourself:
- How do you plan on developing your own feminine genius?
- Think of all the women you know and consider how they use their feminine genius.

"Necessary emphasis should be placed on the 'genius of women', not only by considering great and famous women of the past or present, but also those ordinary women who reveal the gift of their womanhood by placing themselves at the service of others in their everyday lives. For in giving themselves to others each day women fulfill their deepest vocation."

Or, in other words, Pope John Paul II says that it is important to talk, and think, about the "genius of women" (the talents and gifts that God gave women). People should do that by thinking about great and famous women in the past or present, but they should also remember ordinary women who spend their lives in service (helping) others. It is in giving themselves to others that women are able to live their deepest vocation (this means that they are able to fully live out God's calling for them).

Questions you might ask yourself:
- "Ordinary" doesn't sound like a great word; but what does JPII mean when he uses it?
- How can you serve God in your everyday life?
- Why is it important to fulfill your deepest vocation?

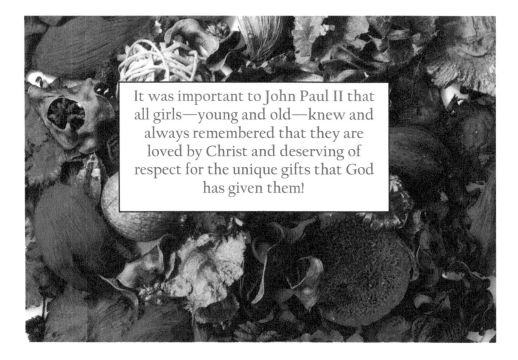

It was important to John Paul II that all girls—young and old—knew and always remembered that they are loved by Christ and deserving of respect for the unique gifts that God has given them!

Me and Social Media

You live in an age where social media abounds! In some ways, that can be a good thing. It is a chance to let people know you love God and you live for His Son, Jesus. On the other hand, it also gives you a chance to be mean to others in ways that are much easier and more hurtful than ever before! Statistics show that young girls spend so much more time in front of their computer, on their iPads or laptops, or just plain texting and instant messaging than ever before...and it probably isn't going to go away.

That is why it is very important for you to take a good, hard, long look and what you do and "say" through social media. Do an Examination of conscience to help get yourself started and to recognize if your habits needs to change or if they are interfering with your relationship with God.

And when in doubt, abstain from social media.

You certainly can't harm others—or your soul—if you aren't spending time in social media!

Here are some Examination of Conscience questions that might help you decide if you are in charge of your media habits or if they are in charge of you:

1. How much time did I spend with media (computer time, texting, watching television and so on) today versus time spent in prayer?
2. Did something I saw in a magazine or on the Internet make me feel like I should look or act a way different than a way befitting a "soulful" person?
3. Did I regularly remember today that I am a daughter of the King and act that way?
4. How did I treat my friends on the Internet today?
5. How did I treat strangers on the Internet today?
6. Did I spend time watching shows that were inappropriate and made me feel less than dignified?

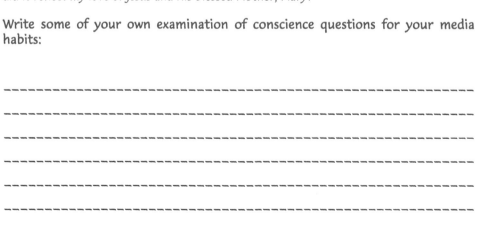

7. Whatever I did today—from watching television to catching up on social media sites—did it reflect my love of Jesus and His blessed Mother, Mary?

Write some of your own examination of conscience questions for your media habits:

Fashion, Skin, Hair, and Makeup

Modesty and the Basics for Looking Good

"How beautiful then is modesty and what a gem among virtues it is."
~ St. Bernard ~

You might be the kind of girl who loves shopping for new clothes! Or, you may not be all that interested in them. Either way, there are some important things that you should think about when you are getting dressed for the day.

Remember, you are a daughter of God! That is pretty amazing, but it's also an awful lot to live up to. God created you to love and serve Him! One way to do that is by making sure that we keep up our physical appearance. That doesn't mean that He wants us to worry about how pretty we look in the mirror, but it *does* mean that He wants us to be neat, clean, and healthy. One way to show the world that we love God, and want Him to be impressed with us, is through what we put on each morning before school (or Mass, or sporting events, etc.).

So, how do we decide what to wear and what not to wear? First of all, it is super important to wear neat, clean clothes. If you own something that is dirty or crumpled up, just put it in your laundry hamper or ask your mom to wash it for you. You should also think about patching up any clothes that you have with holes in them (ask your mom for help!), or donating them to the local St. Vincent de Paul's. If you stain your clothes, you should ask one of your parents to help you get it out. Some stains don't come out, but most do. These tips should help you keep your clothes looking neat and clean!

Another thing to keep in mind is your own personal hygiene. The fact is, you will look much better in that new outfit you just bought if you are staying showered on a regular basis! It doesn't have to be overwhelming to stay on top of your personal hygiene; here are some basic guidelines to follow:

- ✞ Make sure to shower at least every other day, and definitely every time you exercise. Wash behind your ears, too!
- ✞ Wash your hair at least a couple of times every week.
- ✞ Make sure to brush your teeth in the morning and at night.
- ✞ Wear deodorant.
- ✞ Brush your hair every day before school.
- ✞ Wash your face. You can use face wash, or you can just use soap, making sure not to get it in your eyes.
- ✞ Make sure your fingernails don't have dirt trapped underneath them. If you do get dirt stuck underneath your fingernails, don't worry! All you have to do is cut them shorter and wash your hands. The dirt will come right off.

These tips should help you stay looking neat and clean. And as long as you look neat and clean, you will always be fashionable, not only in the eyes of your friends, but also in the eyes of God!

Another thing that you can do to show the world that you are a beloved daughter of God is to make sure that you are wearing modest clothes. You may be wondering what modesty is, exactly. Modesty is a great quality for both girls and guys to have! It means not showing things that are meant to be private. That means that as a modest girl, you should make sure you cover up your private parts. You should not wear a low-cut shirt that people can look down. You also shouldn't wear baggy pants without a belt. You may think that something is fashionable to wear today and then in a year or two find yourself embarrassed that you looked so immodest. A good thing to tell yourself if you are tempted to dress inappropriately is that modesty never goes out of style! You will **never** regret making modest choices.

You want to be respected, don't you? Of course you do! Girls who are respected are liked and admired by their friends, their acquaintances, their teachers, and their coaches. More importantly, it pleases God to see girls whom He can respect! And, in the end, *everyone* respects a modest girl! So, how exactly does a girl gain respect by her clothing choices?

Maybe you think that a girl will only be respected for the clothes she wears if she owns the most popular brand, or has shoes that have been the latest rage. Wrong! Everyone can be respected for the clothing choices that they make, as long as they try to keep their clothes neat, clean, and modest! Try to guess which of the following outfits will get the most respect:

- ✞ A beautiful ball gown
- ✞ A pretty purple shirt, paired with neat, clean jeans
- ✞ Khakis and a red sweater
- ✞ A Hollister sweatshirt and jeans
- ✞ A colorful skirt that is a little past knee-length, and a pretty shirt
- ✞ Torn-up jeans and a paint-smattered t-shirt
- ✞ A plaid mini-skirt and a low-cut shirt

The truth is that all of the outfits listed above - except for the torn-up jeans and paint-smattered t-shirt outfit (too messy) and the plaid mini-skirt and low-cut shirt outfit (not classy and modest enough) are equally worthy of respect. A pretty purple shirt is just as respectable as a *Hollister* sweatshirt—even if the shirt cost a lot less and isn't a brand name. Don't be fooled into thinking you have to wear a logo to be respected. In fact, if you think about it, do you really want to be accepted because of what you wear? Wouldn't you rather be accepted and respected for who you are?

That means that even if you wear the least popular brand of shoes and a skirt that you found at a thrift shop, you will still be respected, just as long as you have chosen modest and pretty clothes! And the same is true for a girl who wears popular clothing brands. If she is making smart, modest choices, she will be respected, too.

The point is that it doesn't matter what brand you're wearing (or even if you wear off-brand clothing), just as long as you look and act like a daughter of God - modest *and* pretty! And, in the end, if you are wearing pretty, modest clothing, your friends and the adults in your life will see *you* as being neat and modest. They will respect you for your grown-up and mature choices. So will God! That's pretty awesome, isn't it? Here are a few rules of thumb to follow if you aren't sure if you are dressing modestly:

- ✞ Never, ever wear see-through clothing. If you do have a semi see-through dress or skirt, you can always buy a slip to wear underneath.
- ✞ When wearing skirts or shorts, make sure that they come down to at least your fingertips (when your arms are down at your sides). For skirts, knee-length or longer is your safest bet.
- ✞ When wearing jeans (or any other kind of pants) that are a little too big for you, wear a belt.
- ✞ Make sure that your shirts are always long enough to cover your belly.
- ✞ Don't wear shirts that are low-cut. This means that anything that is two fingers breadth (two fingers held sideways) below your collarbone is okay, but anything that is lower-cut is not okay.
- ✞ Clothing should never be too tight.

✝ Make sure, if you wear clothes that have logos or words on them, that they are not inappropriate.

Examination of Conscience

If you are unsure if you are really showing love to God by being modest, here is a quick examination of conscience that you can do to check. These are just some basic questions, so if you think of some others on your own, that's great! Ask yourself:

✝ Do I spend too much time in front of the mirror every day?
✝ Do I care more about my appearance (how I look on the outside) than about who I am on the inside?
✝ Do I ever find myself judging others for their physical appearances? For example, do I often look at other people and think to myself, "Wow, that is an ugly outfit that he/she's wearing!" or "At least I look prettier than that!"
✝ Do I pick out new clothes based on how they will reflect my love of God, or do I choose clothes that are revealing or too tight?
✝ Do I wear certain things just to get attention from boys or my friends?

Remember that keeping up your physical appearance *is* important - it is good to shower, to be clean, and to try to look your best! The problem begins if you spend *too* much time in front of the mirror or in the bathroom. When you find yourself thinking more about how you look, and less about God, then you may have to consider changing your habits.

Fashion

Now that you've gotten the basics down, the rest should be pretty easy! Do you ever feel like you're tired of your wardrobe, or need a new way to spice up a favorite outfit? One really great way to solve this problem is by adding *accessories*. Take a look at some of the accessories below, and think of ways that you could match them up with your favorite t-shirt and jeans, or your favorite dress-up outfit!

Jewelry: This is a pretty big category, and involves necklaces, earrings, rings, and bracelets! As long as your mom doesn't have a problem with you wearing jewelry, this can be a great way to add new life to an old outfit. Try some of these tips:

✝ If you have a colored bracelet (or earrings, etc.), try matching it with a shirt or pants/a skirt of the same color. For instance, if you have a red bracelet, it would probably look great with your red shirt!
✝ If you aren't sure how a piece of jewelry will look with your outfit, go ahead and try it on! A lot of times you will be able to tell if something works - or doesn't - just by looking at yourself wearing it. If you're still not sure if it looks good, don't be afraid to ask your mom to help you out. Moms are great at giving advice!
✝ If you just got a new piece of jewelry that you really want to wear, you can also find clothes that will make the jewelry look good! For instance, if you got a new bracelet for your birthday, you could try wearing it with a short-sleeved shirt. That way, people will really be able to notice it! Similarly, if you want to wear a new pair of earrings that you just got, you could try wearing your hair up instead of down. That will draw more attention to the earrings!
✝ If you're wearing solid-colored clothing (that means it's all one color), don't be afraid to wear jewelry that has a fun or a wacky print. For instance, maybe you have a leopard-print bracelet. That might look great with a plain black t-shirt!
✝ The opposite is also true. If you're wearing a fun print, wear solid-colored jewelry. Say you have a pink-and-purple polka-dotted t-shirt. It would probably look great with either a plain purple bracelet or a plain pink bracelet. Try it out!

✧ Don't wear too much jewelry. Keep it simple, fun, and beautiful!

Belts: Belts are great accessories! They can also help you stay modest and keep your pants at waist level if they are a little too big for you. There are many different styles of belts. There are simple black and brown leather belts, for instance. Black is a great color to go with because it matches almost everything! Brown matches quite a few colors as well. But if you're looking to spice up your outfits, you could be looking for something a little more wacky and fun. There are plenty of colorful, fun belts out there, too! Just remember that the same principle applies to belts as it does to jewelry: when you're wearing a solid-colored shirt and pants, you can spice things up a bit by wearing a funky printed belt. And vice versa: if you're wearing a crazy zebra-striped shirt, you may want to stick with a solid-colored belt.

Handbags: You might not have a purse yet, and you probably don't need one. But in case you *do* have one, the good news is that it can help make your outfit more complete and cute!

Scarves: Scarves are a fun way of livening up an outfit. You can always use them to keep warm, too! While wearing scarves, remember the print/solid-color rule. If you're wearing a printed outfit, try to stay away from scarves with prints on them. If you're wearing a solid outfit, try a printed scarf! There are a couple of different ways to wear a scarf:

   ✧ You can wrap the scarf around the front of your neck, and let the ends hang down your back.
   ✧ You can wrap the scarf around your neck multiple times, and wear something over the top to keep it in place.
   ✧ You can tie it like a tie. Ask your dad for help on this one!
   ✧ You can also wear a scarf as a headband or a belt, if you roll it up into a cylindrical shape first.

Whatever you end up doing, have fun with it! Fashion is supposed to be about having fun and being creative. Fashion is a way to express your own personality!

Sunglasses: If it's a sunny day, you can always opt to wear your sunglasses! Sunglasses come in many different styles and colors. Sometimes, if you are far-sighted or near-sighted, you can even get prescription sunglasses! That means that you can wear them like your normal glasses, and still see clearly. Sunglasses are another fun and creative way to make your outfits more interesting and exciting!

Headbands: Like all of the other types of accessories that we've discussed, headbands come in a wide variety of styles and materials. Some headbands are made out of plastic. Some are covered with soft fabrics. Some are decorated with gemstones; others have fake flowers attached. Some are striped, some are flowery, and still others are polka-dotted. When choosing a headband, make sure to find one that feels comfortable and doesn't dig into your scalp. On a side note, it's great to borrow accessories from your friends, but don't borrow headbands or anything that touches somebody else's hair. Lice, a wingless insect, hatch their eggs in hair, and spread through brushes, combs, and other things that touch people's hair. Just to be on the careful side, don't borrow or lend anything that touches hair.

So, now that you know all about the different kinds of accessories you can use to spice up your wardrobe, try your hand at making some of your own jewelry!

Bead Bracelet/Necklace: To make a bracelet or necklace with beads, use an elastic cord or plastic lacing. Choose the beads you want to use, and string them onto the elastic cord/plastic lacing, making sure not to spill them on the floor. Tying a knot in one end of the string, before beading, almost always helps to prevent the beads from spilling onto the floor.

Braided Friendship Bracelet: Another type of jewelry that is pretty simple to make is the braided friendship bracelet. Use three different colors of embroidery floss or yarn. Wrap one color of the embroidery floss or yarn around your wrist. Cut it so that the string is about an inch and a half longer than the amount it takes to wrap around your wrist. Cut two more strings (from different colors), which are the same length. Tie the three strings together, so that the knot is at the top. Finally, braid the strings together. When you get close to the end of the string, tie another knot to make sure that the braiding stays in. Tie the two ends of the bracelet together, and if you want, snip the extra tail off the knot with scissors. You've made a braided friendship bracelet! If you need help with this, or any part of the project, be sure to ask your parents. A good tip for braiding the bracelet is to use a safety pin or tape to attach the knot to a solid surface (i.e. your shoelace or a table). That makes the braiding easier on you!

Puberty

You might be reaching a point in your life when you are noticing changes in your body. First of all, you should know that this is completely normal! In fact, all girls and guys must go through changes to eventually become women and men. This period of time is called *puberty*. For girls, puberty often occurs between the ages of seven and 13, and, for boys, puberty usually occurs a little later.

Puberty is an important stage that everyone has to go through. Girls who go through puberty become women. It is an amazing privilege to become a woman! Women are given the wonderful gift of being able to bear children. Don't you think that's pretty awesome? A woman is able to shelter and feed a baby while it is growing inside of her womb. Once the baby is born, a woman is still able to take care of the baby, nurturing it and helping it grow up to be an amazing daughter or son of God! That is a pretty special privilege that only girls have. God created girls especially for this gift.

All of the changes that your body will go through (or is going through) during puberty are meant to help you become a woman, capable of giving birth and nurturing a child. That's so amazing! It's important for you to know, though, that girls go through different stages of puberty at different ages. Some girls' bodies start changing earlier than others. A lot of girls worry that their bodies are taking too long to change, or that their bodies are changing faster than their friends' bodies. This is not something that you have to worry about, though! There is a big range for when a girl begins to experience puberty. If you ever worry about being slower or faster than your friends at hitting puberty, though, you should *always* feel free to talk to your mom, a trusted adult like your grandmother or aunt, or a doctor about your concerns or feelings. They will be able to reassure you that it is completely normal to grow at different rates. They will also be able to help you with any questions that you may have about the amazing privilege of becoming a woman!

Skin Care

One thing that you might notice as you are going through puberty is that your skin changes. It may become oilier and more difficult to maintain. You may get pimples (small red bumps that hurt when you touch them), or other forms of acne, as well. Pimples occur when extra oil gets built up in your pores. It is completely normal for girls—and boys, too—to have some pimple breakouts throughout their years of puberty. There are several things that you can do to help prevent or control pimples:

1. Wash your face often. Use warm water and antiseptic soap. It is especially important to wash your face after it has been exposed to lots of oils. For example, you should make sure to wash your face every time you wear sunscreen.
2. Drink lots of water throughout the day.
3. Cut down on fatty foods, like cookies, chips, and candy.
4. Make sure you don't pick at your pimples. This often makes the problem worse and could leave you with scars!
5. Eat lots of vegetables and fruits.
6. Try to cut down on caffeine from coffee or caffeinated soda.
7. Wash your pillowcase often and use new, clean towels on your face. So that this doesn't make extra work for your mom you should offer to help with the laundry!

If you have bad pimple breakouts nearly constantly, it may be a good idea to talk to your parents about it. Sometimes acne is a problem that can be treated by medication prescribed by a doctor.

Speaking of skin…Did you know that your skin is the largest organ of your body? It is your first line of defense against illness and infection. It deserves your love and care! Lots of girls like to get tans because they think the deeper tone makes them look good; but getting tanned can sometimes be dangerous. Of course different girls have diverse tolerances to the sun, but you should always be careful to avoid sunburns while playing outside or while you are lounging on a chair with a good book. You need Vitamin D—which comes from spending some time in the sun; but like anything, overdoing it can be harmful. Make sure you and your mom pick out a good sun block (there is a number called "SPF" which stands for Sun Protection Factor) for your time in the sun—enough to let the Vitamin D be manufactured but not too much as to end in a burn after a day outside.

Make a Homemade Mask for Your Face

You can make a mask for your face using common household items. Masks like these can help refresh your skin and help reduce pimples! You may have to ask an adult for help.

You will need: 2 c. water; 1 peach (or a banana will work, as well); 1 t. honey; Dry oatmeal; A spoon or a fork; A small saucepan; A medium bowl; *If you use a banana instead of a peach, skip to step number seven. In this case, you will not need the small saucepan and two cups of water.

Directions:
1. Boil two cups of water in the small saucepan.
2. Once the water is boiling, turn the heat down on the stove so that the water is simmering.
3. Place a peach in the water, and cook it. Remove the peach carefully once its flesh is cooked. (A good tip for telling if it is cooked enough is to poke it with the prongs of a fork. If the flesh is soft, then it's cooked!)
4. Let the peach cool. Remove the skin and the pit of the peach.
5. Mash the flesh of the peach (everything except its skin and pit) with a fork or a spoon in the medium bowl. If you choose to use a banana, mash it up into a paste in the medium bowl.
6. Add 1 teaspoon of honey and mix all ingredients together.
7. Slowly add dry oatmeal to the mixture. You'll need just enough oatmeal to create a paste that will be easy to spread onto your face.
8. Spread the mixture onto your face.

9. Let sit for 15 minutes.
10. Rinse off with cool water.

The oatmeal makes the mixture smooth; the fruit gives your skin a healthy glow, and the honey smells good and helps with pimples! Pretty good for a homemade facial mask, right? Great! Now that you know a couple of tips for keeping your skin clear, let's move onto hair!

Hair Care

One really important way of making sure that you're taking care of your appearance is to make sure that you're keeping your hair clean and healthy. The best way to do that is to wash your hair, at least several times throughout the week. You can wash your hair in the shower, or you can wash it in the sink. Either way will help keep your hair from being greasy.

When washing your hair, you should use shampoo. Squeeze about a dime-size pool of shampoo onto your hand. Massage into your hair. Lather. Rinse thoroughly with water. Different shampoos are available for different kinds of hair and scalp problems. Ask your mom to help you do some research to find the best product for your own circumstances. For instance, if you suffer from dandruff, a tar shampoo might be what you need (it stinks but works!); but if you have curly, coarse hair you may need a shampoo that is creamier and will trap in moisture. Finding out what works best for you can be a fun part of taking care of yourself!

You can also use conditioner. Conditioner helps prevent frizzy or split ends. You do not need to apply conditioner to your scalp. In fact, it is better to apply it to the bottom of your hair and work upwards, to about an inch or two away from your scalp. That's because your scalp produces its own oils. Use about the same amount of conditioner as you would shampoo. Massage it into your hair. Rinse well with cool water. Cool water helps close hair cuticles, so the conditioner stays trapped into your hair. This will help make your hair silky, shiny, and smooth!

Okay, so you've gotten the basics down. But what about blow-drying or straightening your hair? There are some pretty simple tips to help with both of these, too!

When blow-drying your hair, it can help to put some kind of hair serum in your hair. That keeps your hair from getting too frizzy and from getting split ends. It can also help to divide your hair up into layers while blow-drying. Blow-dry the top layer of your hair, clip it up, and then move onto the layer underneath. Keep blow-drying each layer until you've finished.

If you have a hair straightener, and your mom doesn't mind you using it, follow similar tips to the ones above for blow-drying. If your hair is wet, and you want to straighten it, try using hair serum. Divide your hair up into layers, straightening the top layer first, and then all of the layers underneath it. Use pins or clips to help hold the top layers out of your way. If you use a hair straightener, one of the most important things to remember is to not burn yourself!

No matter what, though, you need to make sure you have a good quality hair-cut. Again, learning about yourself can help you make an informed decision. Like many beauty products, a good cut may be worth the investment, especially if you have hard to manage hair and getting professional cut or advice can be the difference between being miserable about your locks and loving them! If this is what you would like to do, make sure your mom knows that you are willing to work towards paying for a professional cut in a salon; but don't assume that this is something you always have to do. Maybe getting a good cut and/or advice can then work for you in a less-expensive salon. Talk all this out with your mom. She's got wisdom and experience that will be worth tapping into and she will appreciate that you are seeking her opinion!

Make-up

You probably see a lot of girls wearing make-up. Celebrities in magazines and on TV wear make-up. Your older sister and her friends might wear make-up. Maybe your mom even wears make-up. Wearing make-up can be a good way to help girls feel good about themselves, but right now, you are probably too young to wear it. Think about it. You are beautiful just the way that God made you! Why would you want to cover that up?

Wearing lip gloss is okay for girls your age, but wearing lipstick and mascara is for older girls. As a modern girl who loves God, you want to be modest, right? One way that girls your age can show their modesty is through their choice not to wear make-up in public until they are a little older and know how to use it in moderation.

That is not to say that you can't experiment with make-up at home, as long as it is fine with your parents. If you really want to practice putting make-up on for when you get a little older, you can ask your parents to see if they mind you having a make-up party with your friends. If you talk to them, and they don't have a problem with it, you can invite a few of your closest girl friends over to have a make-over party. Then you can try lipstick and eye shadow in the comfort of your own home. Just be careful not to share your experimental make-up with your friends, because you can sometimes get sick from sharing lipstick and eye shadow/mascara. If you do have a make-over party, keep in mind that God really did create you (and your friends!) as a beautiful, amazing, and wonderful girl. Make-up can't make you any better than you already are. After all, you are already perfect in God's eyes!

Manners and Etiquette

"Life be not so short but that there is always time for courtesy." -Ralph Waldo Emerson-

Did you know that having good manners is just as important—if not more—than being fashionable? Just like God wants you, as His beloved daughter, to look presentable and modest, He wants you to act in a manner worthy of respect. You may be wondering just how you can do that. One simple way to show God your love is through having good manners! People with good manners treat everyone around them with dignity and respect. They listen carefully when an acquaintance is telling them about his or her day. They say "please" and "thank you" when appropriate. They genuinely care about the feelings of the people around them, and are gentle and kind when dealing with difficult people. So how can you, as a daughter of God, show good manners? Here are a couple of simple tips that can help you become a model of manners:

- ✢ When somebody gives you a present, always tell them "thank you." If you can thank them in person, that's great, but if you can't, you should make sure to send them a thank you card.
- ✢ When requesting a favor from somebody, always begin (or end) with the word "please." Even if you are just asking your little sister to pass you the peas, it's important to say, "Please pass the peas, little sis." She'll appreciate it!

✧ When two friends of yours are meeting each other for the first time, make sure to introduce them to each other. Say, "Jenna, this is Kate. Kate, this is Jenna." This will make them feel more comfortable! You should also do the same for adults that you know. For instance, if your mom is meeting your teacher, it is always nice to say, "Ms. Hall, this is my mom, Mrs. Smith."

✧ When you have hurt someone's feelings, always be ready and willing to tell them that you are sorry. The opposite is also true! If somebody tells you that they are really sorry for something that they've done to hurt you, show your good manners and forgive them. Jesus taught that forgiveness is one of the most important Christian values!

✧ Be a good guest. For instance, if you are eating over at a friend's house for dinner and they are eating cabbage and you really don't like the look or smell of cabbage then you should silently offer up the sacrifice you are about to make and politely dig in with a smile and a fork and eat the food that has been prepared and offered to you!

✧ Speaking of food…always use good table etiquette:
- ♥ Chew with your mouth closed. That means that when you are chewing, you shouldn't be talking!
- ♥ Make sure to keep your elbows off the table.
- ♥ Make sure you don't start eating until everyone has been served. That way everyone who is hungry can eat at the same time!

Manners Quiz

Take this quiz to see where you fall on the politeness scale!

1. When somebody gives you a gift, you thank them in person or send them a thank-you card.
   Almost Always　　　*Sometimes*　　　*Almost Never*
2. When you've hurt somebody's feelings, you tell them that you're sorry.
   Almost Always　　　*Sometimes*　　　*Almost Never*
3. When you ask for a favor from somebody, you use the word "please."
   Almost Always　　　*Sometimes*　　　*Almost Never*
4. You think about how your words will affect the people around you before you say anything.
   Almost Always　　　*Sometimes*　　　*Almost Never*
5. When somebody tells you that they are sorry for hurting you, you try to forgive them.
   Almost Always　　　*Sometimes*　　　*Almost Never*
6. When you need food that's across the table from you, you politely ask somebody to pass it to you.
   Almost Always　　　*Sometimes*　　　*Almost Never*
7. When you are a guest, and your host needs help doing something (like washing dishes), you offer to help.
   Almost Always　　　*Sometimes*　　　*Almost Never*

Great job! Figure out which category you fall into by tallying up your answers and seeing which answer choice you picked the most. Answers are on page 83 of the book.

Financial Responsibility

What is Financial Responsibility?

 Throughout your growing years you should be discerning God's call upon your life. You may be going to college, you may be getting married, or you may be a single woman. Regardless of how you are called, you will be called to financial and fiscal responsibility. This means you ought to be responsible with your money as well as your time and your talents.

Chances are you are already earning money—either through babysitting, or an allowance, or at a part-time job. What are you doing with that money? Are you saving it? Are you giving some to God? Do you have a big purchase in mind—like a cell phone or even a car—for which you are saving some money? What about a "rainy day fund" as the old saying goes—will you be prepared?

Like all the things we've discussed in the book, there's no better time than the present to begin to put good things into action. You are developing a prayer life, you are behaving in a way fitting a soulful daughter of God, and you ought to start being financially responsible with your allowance or the money you are earning at a job. You may have money from things like First Communion or Confirmation. You will probably be getting money for things like high school graduation. Money is going to always be a part of life and you want to start now by understanding it and making good decisions.

There are many ways to go about this—and you should always rely on your mom and dad for guidance—but here are a few things for you to keep in mind as you grow into a beautiful woman ready to serve God.

- *Did you know that kids your age are considered "Consumers?"*
- *Did you know that kids your age are spending more than 180 billion dollars a year on stuff?*

This means lots of kids are spending lots of money and advertisers know it! Big marketing firms want you to spend your money on their things! They will target ads to appeal to you and make you feel you "need to have something" to a point that you may even feel like fighting with your mom or dad about it if they don't agree or approve. You may see these ads on television or in a magazine or on the Internet. The point is there are people that know you have money to spend and they want your money! Now that isn't all bad—people are allowed to make a living, right? But it is important for you to be smart and knowledgeable when you go out into the world with your money.

Some people like to say that the Bible says "Money is the root of all evil," but that is taking it out of context. Taking something out of context means trying to make it mean something it really doesn't; or twisting something someone wrote or said to support your own belief or argument. So it isn't that money is the root of all evil but that how we "use" our money can be wrong—or even evil. God doesn't say we shouldn't have money; but that spending our money and practicing self-control, for instance, is really what we want as our goal.

As you grow and mature as a woman, you will want to be responsible with the money you earn. This means you will create a budget and live within your means. When you honor God with your money you will always be satisfied. This is because God isn't some big ogre in the sky who doesn't want you to have fun; in fact just the opposite is true! He knows what sort of fun is good for you and what sort of "fun" can be harmful. For instance, spending your money on something that your parents disapprove of will never bring you real joy. God knows this, that's why the fourth commandment is that you obey—or honor—your parents. They love you the most and really only want the best for you. If they tell you that buying an iPod is not what you should do, then buying an iPod isn't something you should do. Maybe your parents see a part of your personality that makes them worry that you will spend too much time listening to your iPod and not enough time studying; or maybe they know you will spend too much money downloading things. The point is, parents—or guardians—have their reasons for the decisions they make. They've lived a lot longer than you have!

Spending money wisely is one side of the coin—good pun, right?! The other side of the coin is debt. Do you know what debt is? It is when you spend more money than you have! Lots of adults get into debt. Some of it may be necessary. For instance, most families get a mortgage so that they can have a home. This means they borrow money from a bank or another lending institution and make a significant purchase—people also do this for their cars—and then they make payments to that large institution for the money that was borrowed.

You may be thinking, "Wow, I need to make friends with a large institution so that I can borrow money!" but be warned: those large institutions charge interest for you to "have their money." To make it simple, let's use easy numbers to understand what all this means:

- ✓ You borrow $100 for a bike from your friendly, neighborhood large institution.
- ✓ They charge 10% monthly interest for a year for you to buy that bike. You make monthly payments of $20 for the year and have the bike right away!

That seems cool, right? And in many ways it is, because a lot of the time people do need to use other people's money to get things they need—like a home or a car—but in our example (which is the easiest way to calculate interest and there are many other ways to do it) you would have spent around $140 in a year to have that $100 bike.

So being responsible means practicing self-control as well as being wise about things. Do you need the bike to get to work? Then maybe it would be wise to make that purchase. Is the bike just because your neighbor bought a new bike and you want one, too; but don't really need it because your old bike is actually just fine? Then making the bike purchase isn't wise and certainly isn't showing self-control. Could you find a decent bike at a thrift store or a garage sale for just pennies on the dollar? You get the idea. Having money means looking at the things you do with your money in a smart and virtuous way!

As you get older, this wisdom will help you budget your money. So whether you are a wife and mother or a college student or a single woman with a career, you will always make good money decisions. Here's some brief information about budgets that you may want to tuck away for a rainy day:

A budget is looking at your money and your expenses (the things you have to spend your money on or desire to spend your money on) and making sure that your wants don't overtake your needs!

B = Begin to become familiar with the expenses in your life.
U = Understand where your money is going.
D = Develop a plan.
G = God is at the center of all plans.
E = Execute the plan.
T = Triumph because you have successfully taken control of your finances!

Here are some examples:

Monday: Beauty products $5.00 and Lunch at school $5.00
Tuesday: Dad's birthday $22.00

Once you have started this procedure, you have begun; B has been accomplished. You should track your expense throughout a full month or two to really get an idea of where your money goes. If your mom or dad feels that you waste money, this can give you some insight into your spending habits and help you control them! Tracking your expenses is an ongoing procedure that can really benefit you so you want to continue doing that and keep yourself aware of how you spend your money. That is the "U" as you understand where your money is going and begin to look at that more critically—less emotionally and being able to be more honest with yourself. Being honest about "wants" and "needs" is challenging. But understanding where your money is going is the only way to take control of your finances.

Earlier we mentioned a "rainy day fund". Once you see where you money is going—especially as you get older and have more of it and your expenses increase—you need to make sure you are putting money aside for things that aren't everyday occurrences and so aren't on your "expense radar". That might be purchasing four new tires for your car or contributing to mom and dad's 25th wedding anniversary trip to Italy! The bottom line is that we all need money that has been put away for emergencies or a "rainy day". One important part of your Rainy Day Fund is that you don't take money out of it unless it is a dire emergency. Being able to see your needs and wants clearly can make the difference between using your emergency fund foolishly or wisely!

Always remember that these years—right here, right now—are great prep years to be a responsible, joyful Catholic woman. Why? Because nothing robs us of joy as does debt. This is all part of the "D" in our B-U-D-G-E-T acronym; we are developing a plan for our money. We now need to talk about the letters "G," "E," and "T" because God is part of all plans and it is time to Execute your plan for financial responsibility and experience Triumph!

God should be at the center of your budget because He helps guide you in the ways to practice virtuous living through your money but also because you can give Him money through your Church donations or through ministries that support your Faith. A good suggestion is to give 10 percent to God, whether it is in a weekly contribution to your parish, Right to Life, missionary appeals, Diocesan collections, or any other choices you may have to help others. There are many needs in the church so choose what is important to you.

Tithing isn't just for adults! Tithing is for any Christian who is earning money and is an excellent way to honor God with the fruits of your labor. It may not be easy to get in the habit but remember that diligence and perseverance are key traits that are valued in Scripture. No matter what, the point is to make an effort to live responsibly and know that God is always at the center of what you do. Since we all have many expenses, putting aside 10 percent may not be easy. However, there are endless ways to cut back and this is the best time in life to learn how to do that; but no matter what you do, pray about it and ask God for advice. He will surely guide you.

Here are a couple of suggestions of ways in which you can keep more of your money and have more to give God:

✝ Grow your own plants and give as gifts or offer to clean for your mom for her birthday present or Mother's Day gift.

✟ The next time you get invited to a friend's birthday bash, consider making her a beautiful gift basket filled with things you've made.

✟ There are some excellent clothing buys at thrift stores – don't be embarrassed – check them out!

✟ See if your mom would agree to a clothes swap set up at your house and get some of your friends together who want to "swap" clothes – this gives you new things to wear while not costing a dime – just make sure the swaps are fair and the clothes are clean!

✟ If you eat out, consider giving up one or two of those meals and putting the money you save aside for God.

✟ Spend a day at the spa at home by doing your own manicure and pedicure; do this with your mom or a friend.

Bath Salts

Ingredients and Directions: Epsom salt; Essential oils, such as lavender, or orange food coloring

Mix 1 cup of Epsom salt, ¼ cup sea salt, add 2-3 drops of essential oils, and food coloring to your preference. Add to bath water and enjoy!

Put the colored salt in jars. Decorate the jars with lace, sequins, or beads and give as a gift.

Being financially responsible also means using your dollars wisely from another perspective. We live in a world where "money talks" and you want to make sure that you spend yours in stores or on products that don't ultimately support abortion or other things that are against the Catholic Church. There are many Catholic resources for finding out the real Truth behind such organizations. A great place to start is by checking out the Susan B. Anthony organization. They are committed to helping and supporting pro-life causes.

And a word about time...we've spent a lot of "time" talking about money but time is something you should also be keenly aware of as it is as valuable as money, if not more valuable.

The same sorts of principles that apply to money also apply to time. So, if you feel like you can't get a handle on all the demands of your time, track what you do just like you did with money. Apply the same principles of including God and making Him a top priority. All these things will help you grow into a thoughtful, God-fearing woman whose priorities are right placed and whose life will be lived just as He intended.

This is also the "time" in your life to develop good eating and physical fitness habits. Your body is a temple to the Holy Spirit and to live out your life most fully for God, taking care of your body is important. It isn't about caring for your body in a vain way but caring for your body so that you will be able to be all God wants you to be!

Role Models

Who is Your Role Model?

There are a lot of role models for girls like you to look up to and emulate. Sometimes, though, it gets confusing about what is really, truly important and what are just the things of this world—things which will pass and will not matter for your eternal soul. The Catholic Church has lots of great women in its past to remind you that girls rock! Women like Sarah, Rebekah, Rachel, Leah and Ruth—who is in a story that follows—are just a few from the Old Testament who have made a difference in your faith history. You should never, ever forget that as you go out into the world and encounter many different messages about your worth and your dignity.

> ALWAYS remember that your soul, a gift from God,
> gives you inherent worth and dignity.

God made us in His image and likeness and from the beginning of the human race with Adam and Eve, we were special. Through the Bible, God's word, we also can see that girls rock and that we have a major role to play in the Kingdom of Christ and His plan of salvation. It starts out in the very first book of the Old Testament which says...And I will put enmity between you and the woman and between your offspring and hers; He will crush your head and you will strike his heel.

It was our Blessed Mother's "yes" that we read about in the first chapter of St. Luke's Gospel that allows for Jesus to come into this world and walk and live among us. She said...I am the handmaid of the Lord. Let it be done to me according to thy word.

Other women who lived in Jesus' time also were given important roles to play in God's plan because Jesus treated women with dignity and made them part of His ministry. St. Mary Magdalene, a close friend of our Lord's, was given the amazing privilege of being the first to see the resurrected Lord on that first Easter Sunday Morning. It was Mary Magdalene who was sent to tell St. Peter and the other apostles about the risen Christ.

The many great Catholic saints who have gone before us also remind us that girls do indeed rock. Just like St. Paul tells us in Philippians 4:13: I can do all things in Christ who strengthens me.

So what type of things do you think Jesus is calling you to do and what would you like to do when you grow up? We can be Moms. We can work outside the home and have a family or we can enter the religious life. The possibilities are endless because Jesus loves us. Remember that you are a daughter of the King and the King wants you to have an abundant life.

Sometimes when we watch TV or see a movie or read a magazine, we may notice that girls are made to be objects or that they are being valued only for what they wear or look like, instead of what is in their hearts. Also, the media sometimes may try to give the world the wrong impression that girls have to act a certain way in order to be popular or accepted. But you should never change who you are—and never stop working towards discerning and living the vocation God has in store for you—regardless of how appealing the world's messages may appear. Don't abandon God and His plan for your life!

Always remember that there are great women saints that went before you. One such woman is St Gianna Beretta Molla, a wife, mother, and a doctor. She considered her work her way to serve God and to help heal people both physically and spiritually. St Gianna gave her life for her fourth child. When she learned her pregnancy would be possibly life-threatening she told her husband Pietro that if he had to choose between saving her or the baby, he should save their baby's life.

Another great example for girls was the great St. Catherine of Siena, the patron saint of Italy. St. Catherine died when she was a young woman at only 33 years of age but she played a significant role in bringing the Papacy back to Rome and she also helped to establish peace among the many cities in her country that were torn apart by war. It was St. Catherine who said "when we are who we are called to be, we will set the world ablaze."

St. Thérèse of Lisieux was known for her "little way" which was about small acts of kindness which can lead to holiness when done with great love.

So who are you called to be? Pray and meditate upon that and ask God to show you His will for your life. What talents and interests do you have? These are gifts from God. He would like you to use them for His glory and for His kingdom. Discerning (praying and asking God for guidance) is the perfect place to see where God may be leading you. Don't look to the media or television or Hollywood for answers. Your answers are in following God and saying "yes" just like the Blessed Mother did. Our gifts or talents are given to us by God so we can give back and make a difference and it's never too early to start praying for guidance.

 ## *Role Models Long Ago...*

Many hundreds of years ago there was a woman named Ruth. She was married to one of the sons of Naomi. Naomi was a Jewish woman who loved God so much that she made Ruth see how good it was to love God. Sadly, Naomi's sons died and so did Naomi's husband. This meant that Naomi only had two daughters-in-law left in her family. At that time Naomi was living in a land that was not her home. She was living in a place called Moab and Ruth was from Moab. Ruth was called a "Moabite".

What is so amazing about Ruth's story was that she was considered an "outsider". Because she didn't, at first, believe in the one true God, people didn't think of her as belonging to their crowd or culture. But remember that Naomi was a great witness to Ruth. This means that Naomi lived her life in such a way as people could look at her and sort of see a "walking Bible".

Anyhow, once Naomi's sons died, Naomi encouraged her daughters-in-law to stay in their homeland of Moab but that she, herself, was going to return to her own homeland, Bethlehem. Naomi and her family had left Bethlehem because of a famine but now word was out that there was food in the land so she was going to go home.

Travelling back then was not like it is today. There were no planes to board and no busses or cars. Travel took weeks and months and was very difficult. So, when Naomi announced that she would go back to Bethlehem, it was quite surprising for Ruth to insist on going with her. Not only was it going to be a long and rough trip, but Ruth really wouldn't be welcomed in Bethlehem because she was an outsider. But Ruth couldn't be deterred. That means she couldn't be held back from doing what she wanted to do which was stay with her mother-in-law, Naomi.

This is what Ruth said to Naomi...Do not ask me to abandon or forsake you! For wherever you go I will go, where you lodge I will lodge, your people shall be my people, and your God my God. Wherever you die I will die and there be buried. May the Lord do so and so to me, and more besides, if aught but death separates me from you! *Ruth 1:16*

Wow, those are pretty powerful words, aren't they? Can you imagine how Naomi must have witnessed to Ruth to make Ruth so in love with Naomi's God, your God? But the story gets even better. Once Ruth and Naomi were back in Bethlehem, Ruth met a man named Boaz. He was a distant relative of Naomi's and looked upon Ruth with love. He wanted to marry her and when he made his intentions known all his friends and family gave him their blessings. This is what they said...May the Lord make this wife come into your house like Rachel and Leah, who between them built up the house of Israel. May you do well and win fame in Bethlehem. *Ruth 4:11*

Ruth and Boaz's story is one of real true love and also the story of Jesus. Why? Because Ruth and Boaz had a son they named Obed. Obed then grew up and had a son named Jesse. Jesse is the father of David who became king and is the family tree in which Jesus Christ is born!

Ruth and Naomi are wonderful role models for you. You may never have to make such difficult decisions as they did—or experience such tragedy; but they show how important it is to live for God and let others know how much you love Him!

> The mission of Christ and the Holy Spirit is brought to completion in the Church, which is the Body of Christ and the Temple of the Holy Spirit. *CCC #737*

Do you know these role models? (Answer Key is located in the back of the glossary.)

Margaret Clitherow; St. Lydia; St. Genevieve; Henriette Delille; St. Elizabeth of Portugal; St. Juliana of Liege

1. She was African descent and born in New Orleans. She was a free Black woman during the years before the American Civil War. She gave up her life of ease and wealth for a life of poverty. She founded the Sisters of the Holy Family and endured ridicule, poverty and hard work. The sisters taught poor slave children, and performed other works of charity. She is

   _____

2. She was born in Nanterre, France, and consecrated by St. Germanus. She entered the religious life when she was 15 years old. Later, when Attila's Huns planned to attack the city of Paris, she counseled the Parisians to stay put and pray to be spared from the attack. The Huns changed their plan of attack, and the city was saved. She is _____.

3. She was the first woman to die during the persecution of Catholics in Protestant England. During this time, churches were burned, priests and nuns killed, and many faithful Catholics were thrown into prison to be executed later. She hid priests and held Mass in secret. Without her and others like her, the Catholic Church in England today would not exist. She is

   _____

4. She was St. Paul's first known convert. Born in Lydia, she was a businesswoman who traded purple-dyed goods. When she met St. Paul, she responded positively to his teachings. She allowed him to baptize her entire household. She was also visited by him and St. Silas soon after they escaped from jail. She later inspired St. Brigid of Ireland. She is _____.

5. She was a European Queen, and eventually joined the Third Order Franciscans. This saint said the Divine Office daily, fasted often, and was devoted to helping the poor and the sick. Late in his life, she finally reformed her immoral husband, King Denis. After her husband died, and her son Alphonso was crowned King, she joined the Third Order Franciscans to quietly help the poor for the rest of her life. She is _____.

6. She was an Augustinian nun who had visions of a moon with a diagonal stripe across it. She came to the conclusion that the visions were meant to show that the Church was lacking a very important feast day—a feast day for the Blessed Sacrament. When she finally told her confessor about these visions, he told the bishop, who decided to trust her visions and to institute a feast honoring the Blessed Sacrament, now known as the Corpus Christi feast. She is _____.

Virtues to Live By

Virtues

A virtue is an habitual and firm disposition to do the good. This is what the *Catechism of the Catholic Church* teaches. According to the Catechism, this disposition (this part of who we are) to do the good has a lot of benefits. For example, a person practicing the habit of living a virtuous life will perform good acts and will give the best of herself.

And if you think about it, isn't that what God wants all along? For you to do good things and to give the best of yourself? What's more, the Catechism says that a virtuous person pursues good and chooses it! This means that a person just doesn't do good when she has to make a decision about something where one choice would be good and another not so much; but it means that she actually seeks opportunities to do good!

Think about it.

You and your sister are about to get in a fight over whose turn it is to take the laundry to the washer. Doing good means that before you open your mouth to yell or scold or tattle you stop and think, *"Hmmm, will it be so bad if I take this even if it is not my turn?"*

That's nice because maybe your mom really isn't up to listening to a fight between you and sis.

But being a virtuous person is even more than that! It is when you don't wait until it boils down to a near-fight; instead it means that you keep an eye on the laundry and when it is getting close to the top of the hamper and you say to yourself, *"Okay, this would be helpful to my mom if I took this to the washer without being asked and without bickering with my little sister."* And then you do it!

You see the difference?

They are both good things that you've done but one is even better than the other.

You see, the Catechism says that *"The goal of a virtuous life is to become like God."*

Now taking the laundry to the washing machine may not seem very God-like; but it is in doing even the smallest things with a pure heart that will continue to help you grow in virtue. Today it is the laundry and tomorrow it is spending time with a sick neighbor who has never been nice to you. The more you do for God, the more you are able to for God!

It sounds a bit crazy, but it is true. That's because each step that has a bit of difficulty in it is a step you are taking for God and He will give you the grace and strength to take the next step. This is really what walking with God is all about— and you want to live in a way that you always walk with God. That is why sin is so terrible. Sin moves you away from God, not closer. And just like God will give you strength each time you take a step for Him and with Him; it is important to remember that the opposite is true. So if you've sinned, you will see that unless you go to Confession (the Sacrament of Reconciliation), it will become easier and easier to sin. Not good, right?

But let's get back to talking about virtues.

As you grow, certain virtues will become very important to you. For instance, there is a virtue called "prudence," which will help you make good decisions about things. Like all the virtues, the more you practice them, the better you will get.

Let's look at an example of being prudent.

Sarah wanted to help feed the poor in her city. She rounded up some friends and they had a few canned food drives to collect food but also had a huge neighborhood garage sale to which everyone donated many great items. The neighborhood garage sale was a great success and a few hundred dollars was collected. Sarah was beside herself with giddiness as she held the money in her hand. After counting it, she kept repeating the words: three hundred and eighty seven dollars! She could hardly believe she held that much money in her hands. Sarah's mother had promised to drive Sarah and Martha to the grocery store once the sale was over, and did just that.

On the way to the store, Sarah and Martha continued to thank God for the success of the garage sale and to help guide them in making good choices with the money that had been earned. Once at the store, Sarah felt that the money could really buy some awesome food, maybe food that the poor at the shelter had not had in a while—or ever. Sarah was tempted to buy the gourmet food but made the prudent decision to purchase cans of tuna, peanut butter, and different cheeses. While it would be fun to have splurged on lobster and steak, it was a wiser decision for Sarah to spend the money so that she could get more food for the money.

You see, Sarah had a huge heart and really wanted to do something special, but prudence helped her make a better decision with the money that had been entrusted to her. Prudence is a virtue that helps you keep things in balance and be a reasonable person but it doesn't mean that you should live without passions and dreams! Prudence is just a way to make sure that your emotions don't rule what you do. Emotions have their place in life—they make things exciting and give you passion to do things; but they shouldn't "rule the roost". That means that your passions should be used for good but sometimes have to be checked. Temperance is a virtue that also helps you keep a good balance with your emotions.

Another virtue that will be important for you to learn, develop, and practice is fortitude. Fortitude is great because it sort of "steels you up" for when the going gets tough! When you have fortitude you are able to resist temptation better and conquer fears. Of course this all means it strengthens you for when you are trying to get past obstacles that are in your way for leading a moral life; remember that the goal of a virtuous person is to become like God. Not in an absurd, egotistical way but in the way of holiness and love. Don't pat yourself on the back if you have fortitude for doing the wrong thing. No way is that what being virtuous is all about!

Cassie's story; a closer look at fortitude...

Cassandra has gotten into lots of trouble in the school year. It started out with a small fight with her mom about a super-short skirt Cassie wanted to borrow from Margie and wear. The tension between Cassie and her mom only got worse from that point on. They seemed to bicker and argue about everything. Cassie was letting her emotions "rule the roost" and was having a difficult time not being mad at her mom, even though she knew it was wrong.

The skirt—which started it all—belonged to Margie and Margie teased Cassie about listening to her "old fashioned" mother. Cassie was embarrassed about Margie's teasing but didn't know how to stay friends with Margie—who was so cool!—while still obeying her mother's adamant "No!" to the skirt.

Cassie went to school with the skirt in her purse and told her mom that she was returning it to Margie that day. Instead, Cassie slipped into the bathroom immediately upon entering school and changed into the super-short skirt. Cassie thought she would feel great as she walked down the hall to class but felt terrible—even some of the boys winking at her didn't make her feel better. In fact, much to her surprise, Cassie felt worse! Her stomach hurt and she wanted to leave her Algebra class and change back into her boring clothes.

As luck would have it, there was no time that day to change back into her khaki Capri pants and Cassie suffered through the longest day of her life wearing the shortest skirt known to man. Cassie couldn't even enjoy lunch time because she couldn't figure out how to sit comfortably. It seemed that every small turn she made to talk to a friend—a real friend and not a "friend" like Margie—caused her skirt to ride up even more. Cassie was sure she was going to die from embarrassment and shame.

By the time the day finally ended, Cassie missed the bus because the lines to the bathroom were so long and she needed to get out of the skirt and give it back to Margie. Cassie walked home to find her mother frantic. Cassie thought that her mother's worry would be a great opportunity to say, "See, that's why I need a cell phone," but she thought better of it and kept her mouth shut while her mother ranted and raved—half in anger and half in relief that Cassie was okay.

To make matters worse, Cassie had to lie to her mom about why she missed the bus. After all, what was she going to say? *"I missed the bus because I wore Margie's skirt all day and needed to get out of it and return it to her."* No, lying seemed better.

If it was possible for the day to get any worse, dinner proved that all things actually are possible. Cassie had no appetite which only caused her father to question how that could be, after all, Cassie was the biggest eater in the house! Or at least that was the family joke. Since Cassie had entered puberty it just seemed as if her stomach was always growling for more and being on the soccer team only increased her voracious appetite.

By the time Cassie fell into bed, she was pleading with God for help. She was more than a bit convinced that even this terrible situation for Him was too big but she relied on faith and hope that all she had learned about God was true and that somehow He could help.

Cassie woke at about 2:30 a.m. with her heart pounding and her nerves frayed. She knew what she had to do but couldn't even imagine how she would do it. First, she had to tell her mom what she had done. Yep, Cassie knew that she had to tell her mom that she wore the skirt and then compounded the sinful disobedience by lying. Cassie spent the rest of the night trying to formulate the words she would use. In between writing the script in her head, Cassie's pleading to God changed to asking for forgiveness. Nothing about her felt good and she knew this is what sin did—it changed you, it separated you from God and from the people you loved. Cassie never wanted to feel this way again. Second, Cassie knew she need to go to confession.

We can learn a lot from Cassie's story.

We can imagine how easy it was for her to succumb to (give in to) temptation and once tempted, see how difficult it is to get back on the right track.

How do you think the conversation between Cassie and her mother would have gone? If you imagine the worse, you should also know that it would be the virtue of fortitude that would have given Cassie strength to have that conversation. In fact, all along, with each step, Cassie is making choices to turn towards God or away; but it is very, very important to also know that at any point in time, we can always repent! God will always take us back. It is never too late to return to Him—regardless of how bad we feel we've sinned or how terrible we feel.

This is also why it is important to see that Cassie knew she needed to receive the Sacrament of Reconciliation. To "reconcile" is to make things better. We see a priest for this because he makes sure we are really freed from our sin because he is standing in the place of Jesus for us. The priest makes sure we get to the bottom of things and helps us get back on the right track. Look at it this way: if we decide on our own we are sorry and then try to avoid receiving the Sacrament of Reconciliation because we are too embarrassed to tell the priest, we can't really be sure we've confessed our sins fully or correctly. After all, didn't we just convince ourselves that sinning was okay? If we are able to do that, how can we assume we can confess rightly without a priest helping us? We can't!

So fortitude once again becomes our friend and gives us the strength to overcome our shame and get to confession. We are persevering towards what is good and right, even if it isn't easy.

See how virtues work? The more we practice them, the better we get at them. Those are called "human virtues" because they are part of us being human and are within our reach. The human virtues sort of rest on what are called "Theological Virtues." Those are virtues given to us by God that are held in the depths of our heart. Theological Virtues are Faith, Hope, and Charity.

Virtues are ways that we work *with* God *and towards* God.

Write a few Examination of Conscience questions to help you see if you are living a virtuous life:

_____

_____

_____

_____

_____

_____

_____

_____

Growing into a Woman with Modesty and Manners

As you continue to grow into the young woman that God intends, it is important that you always remember that manners and modesty are an important part of being a young woman of Christ. Practicing modesty and manners is a virtuous way to live. Remember that what we learned from Cassie's story is that you are not an item on display to be gawked at, or stared at, or judged for your appearance. You are not meant to talk with rude or unacceptable language. You are a precious daughter of the King.

In this media-saturated culture, that statement can sometimes be a tough one to remember **and** to live up to. Have you ever heard the phrase "objectification of women" or just the word "objectification?" The phrase, and the word, means to be treated as an object, or a thing, that is used by someone. Think how sad that sounds: "used" by someone. Do you want to be "used?" Do you want to "use" others? Of course not!

But, unfortunately because of all the pressure in today's culture which stresses appearance over soul and substance, more and more young women (all of whom are created in the image and likeness of God) are allowing themselves to be used. This will **always** make them feel less than dignified. Women are not meant to be valued only in regards to how they dress or how they act around boys.

You are to be valued as a person with a soul and shouldn't expect or accept less!

You are meant to be valued for being created in the image and likeness of God!

Blessed John Paul II was worried by a trend which showed a great disrespect for women and did not reflect how Jesus viewed His precious daughters. JPII wrote:

> When it comes to setting women free from every kind of exploitation and domination, the Gospel contains an ever relevant message which goes back to the attitude of Jesus Christ himself. Transcending the established norms of his own culture, Jesus treated women with openness, respect, acceptance and tenderness. In this way he honored the dignity which women have always possessed according to God's plan and in his love.

These are important words for you to remember.

Blessed John Paul II wanted every female to know that Jesus treated women with "openness, respect, acceptance, and tenderness".

In Chapter 4 of St. John's Gospel, Jesus meets the Samaritan woman at the well. He restores her dignity by telling her about the "living water" only He can give. St. Martha and St. Mary or, the 'Women of Bethany' as they are also known, became a key part of His ministry, along with St. Mary Magdalene. Did you know that St. Mary Magdalene was the first to see our risen Lord on the very first Easter Sunday? Maybe this doesn't sound so impressive to you because you are blessed to live during a time where women and girls have all kinds of different opportunities. But in Jesus' day it certainly wasn't the case. As a matter of fact women were considered property and if you needed a witness in a court of law only the testimony of men was allowed! That's why Jesus thought it was so important for EVERYONE to understand that God created women with great dignity and value. We don't want our world going back to the time before Jesus when women were often objects and not daughters of the King.

The Bible and the Catholic Church uphold our dignity and also teach us that our bodies are temples of the Holy Spirit.

One important key to your own dignity is how you dress and how you speak to people. Your outside should reflect your inside and should show the world that you value yourself enough to dress modestly and to conduct yourself with manner appropriate for a young woman with a soul given to her by God! Your clothing should reflect that you know what it means to be a daughter of the King.

A great way to know that you are growing into the young woman God intends is to do an Examination of Conscience for your manners and your modesty. Some questions that you might ask yourself include:

✝ Do I speak rudely to my parents, friends, teachers or siblings?
✝ Did I gossip today or spread rumors?
✝ What did I say today that might have offended our Blessed Mother or her Son, Jesus?
✝ Did I fight with my parents or guardians about clothes that I wanted to wear?
✝ Do my clothes reflect that I am a dignified person or do they reflect that I want to be "objectified?"
✝ Would Jesus be proud of me today because of the way I dressed and talked?

Vices: The Opposite of Virtues

So if virtues are habits of good actions and habits, what are we doing when we aren't living virtuously? Well, chances are we may be practicing bad habits—or what are often called "vices". Vices are the opposites of virtues. Vices can lead us into sin and so we ought to be very careful of them.

Here's sort of how it can happen:

One day your mom asks you a simple question, "Did you finish your homework?" Even though you didn't finish it, you know it will be easier to just say "yes," and so you do. After you tell that little white lie to avoid upsetting your mom, you quickly go and finish your homework.

The next week your mom calls you from work and asks you another simple question, "Did you do all your chores?" Even though you didn't do all your chores, you know that if you say "yes" that you can quickly get them finished before she gets home from work and she'll never really know. You hang up the phone and quickly finish your chores before she opens the front door. You are quite proud of yourself and how you've saved your mom from being upset!

You are starting to convince yourself that your lying isn't wrong because it actually "helps your mom not be mad"; but the reality is that you are also lying to yourself, too! You are developing vices that are leading you to sin. And sooner or later it begins to get easier to sin—just like it became easier to lie!

There are two types of sin: venial and mortal. Mortal sins are serious offenses against God and they destroy virtues within us—like charity—that help us love God, ourselves, and others. Mortal sins completely separate us from God.

Venial sins are considered less serious than mortal sins because they don't completely separate us from God, but they do harm our relationship with Him. Think about it; if you have a friend who doesn't respect you and is lying to you, how will you feel about her? It changes the relationship you have with her. If she does something really, really bad you might have to make the difficult decision that you can no longer be friends with her. In a way, that is what happens with the two types of sins and how they affect our relationship with God.

So, if you have committed any sin you need to get to confession. You must receive the Sacrament of Reconciliation and get back on the road to God.

No matter what you have done, God is there for you. He just wants you to turn to Him with a loving heart and a sincere wish to be the best you can be. But remember: God can't be fooled; you can't tell the priest (who is sitting in for Jesus) that you are sorry for, say, gossiping, if you know that once you leave the confessional you are probably going to go gossip to your friends. You have to make a real and honest effort to change your ways. If you do that, you can be assured that God is full of love and mercy and forgiveness so that you can get on with your life. He's that amazing.

A Prayer Life

Prayer Life

For me, prayer is a surge of the heart; it is a simple look turned toward heaven, it is a cry of recognition and of love, embracing both trial and joy.
~ St. Therese of Lisieux

So, Why Is Prayer Important, Anyway?

Did you know that St. Therese of Lisieux was fifteen when she joined the Carmelite Convent? She had to ask for special permission to join the convent early, but she did it anyway. That's because she wanted to have a very special relationship with God and Jesus Christ. She was so excited to live out a life of prayer that she even went to the Pope to ask for this special permission! Now, you may be wondering why prayer is so important, and why St. Therese of Lisieux was so excited about it.

Prayer is important because it allows us to have a meaningful relationship with God. You think that it is important to have a good relationship with your friends and family members, don't you? Well, it is just as important for you to have a healthy relationship with God as it is to have a good relationship with your family and your friends!

Now, think about it. How do healthy human relationships work? We communicate with one another. We talk to our friends or family members about all of the good things that have happened to us throughout the day. The same can be true with God! Sometimes a prayer to God can be as simple as telling Him about all of the wonderful parts of your day—from the great softball game you played to a fun evening that you had with your friends—and thanking Him for them!

But what if you're having a really bad day, and can't think of many positives to thank God for? Well, for starters, you can always thank Him for the basic things that He gives us. He gives us life! That's a pretty awesome thought. He also gives us friends, family members, and good food to eat. If we remember that even the simple good things in our lives are gifts from God, then it becomes easy to thank Him!

Prayer also doesn't always have to be about the good things that are happening in your life. Think about it. When you are talking to your best friend, do you only ever tell her about the great test grade that you just got, or how your audition for the school play went wonderfully? Of course you don't. You also talk to your friends and family members about the bad things that are happening in your life. Maybe your grandma is really sick, or maybe you didn't make the try-outs for the basketball team. Your friends and family members are there for you when these things happen. They listen to what you have to say, and try to comfort you. The same is true with God. You can always bring your problems to God. He loves you more than you can imagine. When you are having trouble, He wants to hear all about it so He can help you fix it.

So, prayer is important because it helps us communicate with God and get closer to Him. When you pray, you can talk about how your day is going—the ups and downs, and all of the things that worry you. God loves to hear you tell Him about yourself, because He loves you. Since God loves you, He wants to learn all about you!

If you had a really boring day, and can't think of anything to pray about, you can always pray for other people, too! Maybe your brother isn't doing very well in school. You can pray for him! Or maybe your two best friends have gotten into a fight and are no longer speaking to one another. You can pray to God for them, too! God always hears our prayers.

I Know It's Important to Pray, but Sometimes It Just Seems Hard!

Maybe you already know that it is important to pray, but you seem to just let the days slip by without getting some prayer-time in. Don't worry! You're not alone. A lot of people struggle with praying every day. Here are some of the things that can make it difficult to pray:

- ⚬ Lack of Time: Sometimes it just seems like there isn't enough time in the day to pray. You get up early in the morning, spend most of the day at school, and then have sports practices or piano lessons or homework to do. Then, before you know it, it is nighttime, and time for bed! This is actually a problem that a lot of people face, even adults. But there are some simple strategies that you can use to make sure that you get a little prayer-time in every day.
  - o Set aside a special time of the day in order to pray. Maybe it's easiest for you to pray in the morning. This is true of a lot of people. When you get up in the morning, you can say a simple prayer to thank God for the new day and to ask Him for any help that you think you could use throughout the day. Maybe you're not a morning person, though. In that case, maybe it's easiest for you to pray right before you go to bed. If you pray before you go to bed, you can thank God for the day that you had, discuss any problems that you experienced, and ask Him to make tomorrow a good day. But whatever works best for you—prayer in the morning, afternoon, or evening—do remember that setting aside a certain amount of time a day for prayer is very important.
  - o Remember that prayers don't always have to be super long, and that you can pray anywhere. For example, maybe God has blessed you with a good grade on a test at school. When you get the test back, you can say, "Thank you, God! I was really worried about this test, but I did just fine on it!" This prayer is really simple and only takes a couple of seconds, but because you are lifting your thoughts up to God, it counts as a prayer!

- ✪ Distractions: Maybe you don't suffer from not having enough time to pray. Maybe you are just too distracted to pray. Luckily, this can be a pretty simple fix.
  - o Go to a quiet place to pray. Sometimes it's hard to pray if there is too much noise going on around us. If we turn off our iPod and the TV and go to a quiet place, it is often much easier to pray. Your bedroom is often a great place to pray. If you go into your room and close your door, then it will be harder for siblings to distract you. But maybe you share a bedroom with your younger sister, and don't think that it's quiet enough. If that's the case, then maybe you can go outside to find a quiet place to pray. Or maybe you could try the basement. But it's important to be in a quiet place in order to have a good conversation with God!
  - o Go somewhere where you can be alone. This is connected to the strategy listed above. If you want to have a really great conversation with God, sometimes it's easier to be somewhere alone.
- ✪ Fear of Praying Wrongly: Sometimes people are afraid to pray just because they think they might be doing it wrong. But this just isn't true! There is no way to pray wrongly.
  - o If you are nervous about praying on your own, then there is a great solution: the Catholic Church has many prayers that are already written down for you to use. If you don't feel like you are ready to pray in your own words, there are lots of prayers out there that are already written down for you! You can pray the *Our Father, the Hail Mary,* or the *Glory Be.* You can even pick up the Bible and read a few verses. When you think about what those verses are about, and what they have to do with your life, you are doing a form of prayer called meditation! That's pretty cool, and pretty simple.
  - o Remind yourself that God is like your best friend. Your best friend isn't going to tell you that you're talking to him or her wrong; that's just ridiculous! Neither is God. Sometimes people think that when you pray, you have to sound like a book. But the truth is that you just have to talk to God like He is your best friend, because He is!
  - o Remember that you pray all of the time and you really have a lot more practice at it than you think! You probably pray before meals, or with your family. And you definitely pray when you go to Mass! So, don't be intimidated. You pray all of the time already!

When you feel like something is getting in the way of praying, these simple tips might be able to help you out!

What Are Some Examples of Prayers We Can Use?

Sometimes it can be easy to think that there is nothing left to pray about. That's why we are so lucky to be Catholics! There are so many different types of prayers that Catholics can use. Here is a look at some of the ways we can pray as Catholics:

Going to Mass

Did you know that going to Mass is a form of prayer? Pope Paul VI once said that "Mass is the most perfect form of prayer!" That's pretty powerful stuff. So, when you go to Mass every Sunday, what you are really doing is praying the most powerful kind of prayer in the world! You are supposed to go to Mass every Sunday and on Holy Days of Obligation, but did you know that you can go to Mass every single day if you want to? That means that you can pray the most powerful form of prayer *every day* if you want to! That's pretty cool.

Praying the Our Father

The Our Father is a pretty important prayer! Jesus Christ actually taught us how to pray the Our Father. You can read about it in the Bible, too:

> "[Jesus said] 'This is how you are to pray:
> Our Father in heaven,
> hallowed be your name,
> your kingdom come,
> your will be done,
> on earth as in heaven.
> Give us today our daily bread;
> and forgive us our debts,
> as we forgive our debtors;
> and do not subject us to the final test,
> but deliver us from the evil one'" (Matt. 6:9-13).

Because the Bible has been translated into English, there are a couple of different translations of the *Our Father*. You can pray the version that you know best. The *Our Father* is also known as the *Pater Noster*, which is Latin!

Praying Other Vocal Prayers

There are other prayers that are already written down that you can pray as a Catholic. Some of these include: the *Hail Mary* (also known as the *Ave Maria*), the *Glory Be* (also known as the *Gloria*), the *Nicene Creed* (which is prayed at Mass), the *Act of Contrition* (which is prayed during confession), the *Hail, Holy Queen* (also known as *Salve Regina*), and the *Guardian Angel Prayer*.

The Rosary

One of the coolest prayers that Catholics get to pray is the rosary! The rosary is a good way to think about all of the parts of Jesus' life—from his birth to his resurrection—and is also a good way to honor His mother, the Virgin Mary.

Depending on what day it is, you can reflect on different parts of Jesus' life. These different parts of Jesus' life are divided up into *mysteries*. There are four types of mysteries: the Glorious Mysteries, the Joyful Mysteries, the Luminous Mysteries, and the Sorrowful Mysteries.

The Glorious Mysteries

During Ordinary Time, the Glorious Mysteries are prayed on Sundays and Wednesdays. They include:

1. **The Resurrection of the Lord** ~ This is when Jesus rose from the dead and appeared to his mother and his disciples for forty days.
2. **The Ascension of the Lord** ~ This is when Jesus went up to Heaven to be with God.
3. **The Descent of the Holy Spirit at Pentecost** ~ This is when the Holy Spirit descended on Mary and the Apostles, in the form of fire.
4. **The Assumption of Mary into Heaven** ~ After the Virgin Mary died, she was taken, body and soul, into Heaven to be with God for eternity. This is called "the Assumption."
5. **The Coronation of Mary as Queen of Heaven and Earth** ~ This is when the Virgin Mary was crowned as a Queen of both Heaven and Earth.

The Joyful Mysteries

During Ordinary Time, the Joyful Mysteries are prayed on Saturdays and Mondays. They include:

1. **The Annunciation of Gabriel to Mary** ~ This simply refers to when the angel Gabriel spoke to the Virgin Mary about her becoming the mother of Jesus. Gabriel's first words to Mary were, "Hail, full of grace." These words are also the beginning of the Hail Mary!
2. **The Visitation of Mary to Elizabeth** ~ Do you remember how Mary visited her cousin, Elizabeth, after she received the news that she would be the mother of Jesus? When Mary met her cousin, the baby in Elizabeth's womb leapt for joy because he knew that Jesus was near!
3. **The Birth of Jesus** ~ You probably remember the story of Jesus being born in a manger! It's pretty amazing to think that the King of the world was born in such a humble way, isn't it?
4. **The Presentation of Jesus in the Temple** ~ According to Jewish custom, boys like Jesus had to be presented at the temple. Mary was obedient to the Jewish laws/rules by presenting her son at the temple.
5. **The Finding of Jesus in the Temple** ~ When Jesus was twelve years old - not that much older than you! - He visited a temple with his parents. Mary and Joseph left the temple, not realizing that Jesus was still there. They couldn't find Him for three whole days! Can you imagine how worried they must have been? But Jesus was right where God wanted Him to be. He was praying!

The Luminous Mysteries

During Ordinary Time, the Luminous Mysteries are prayed on Thursdays. They include:

1. **The Baptism of Jesus in the River Jordan** ~ Do you remember the story of Jesus getting baptized in the River Jordan? He had John the Baptist, the son of Mary's

cousin Elizabeth, baptize Him, even though John the Baptist didn't think he was worthy to baptize the Lord.

2. *The Wedding at Cana* ~ This was Jesus' first miracle! This is when Jesus turned the water into wine at his friends' wedding feast.
3. *The Proclamation of the Kingdom of God* ~ This is when Jesus came to Galilee and taught about Heaven, especially about how to get there.
4. *The Transfiguration of Jesus* ~ Do you remember the story of Jesus climbing a mountain with Peter, James, and John? When they reached the top, Jesus' clothes became dazzling white, and both Elijah and Moses appeared. This was the Transfiguration of Jesus!
5. *The Last Supper and the Holy Eucharist* ~ This is when Jesus had His Last Supper with His Apostles. He took the bread and broke it, and told His Apostles that it was His body, and that they were to eat it. Then He took a cup and told His Apostles that it was His blood, and that they were to drink of it. This is where we get the Holy Eucharist at Mass!

The Sorrowful Mysteries

During Ordinary Times, the Sorrowful Mysteries are prayed on Tuesdays and Fridays. They include:

1. *The Agony of Christ in the Garden* ~ This is when Jesus was thinking about He had to be crucified on the cross so that we could be saved. He prayed to God about it, because He was scared. But even though He was scared, He told God that He would do whatever God asked Him to do. That's pretty amazing!
2. *Jesus Is Scourged at the Pillar* ~ This is when the soldiers hurt Jesus by whipping Him.
3. *Jesus Is Crowned with Thorns* ~ This is when the soldiers put a crown of thorns on His head to make fun of Him and mock Him.
4. *Jesus Carries His Cross* ~ This is when Jesus carries His cross up the hill. Do you remember that He fell three times on the way up?
5. *The Crucifixion of Jesus* ~ This is when Jesus was nailed to the cross and died.

When you pray the rosary, you think about these different parts of Jesus' life. You also honor Jesus' mother, the Virgin Mary. It's a pretty awesome kind of prayer that only Catholics have!

Eucharistic Adoration

Catholics also have a really cool type of prayer that Protestants don't have. They get to go to Eucharist Adoration! Now, this can sound intimidating, but it really isn't. Do you remember how when you go to Mass, the bread turns into the body of Jesus, and the wine turns into His blood? This is called transubstantiation. When a host (the bread) is consecrated (that means that the priest uses a special blessing to ask God to make it into Jesus), then Jesus is right there! So a consecrated host (what looks like the piece of bread you eat every Sunday at Mass), is actually Jesus! I know, amazing, right? He is actually there! Sometimes churches will put out a host like this, just so you can pray in Jesus' presence. Think about it. You are lucky enough to be able to pray with Jesus *right in the same room as you.* That's so awesome. When you go to Eucharistic Adoration, you can kneel, or *genuflect,* like you do at Mass towards the host. Then, you can just sit there and pray. You can pray any of the prayers that we've already talked about, or you can just sit there and talk to God about your day.

Sometimes people even just go to sit and look at Jesus. You can also take a book with you that will help you think about the sacrifice Jesus made for you. A great book to take is *Walk New* by Kathryn Mulderink. It has the Stations of the Cross with explanations, beautiful pictures drawn by Father Kynam, and simple meditations for each station.

Reading the Bible

Did you know that when you read the Bible, you are actually reading the inspired word of God? That means that the people who wrote the Bible were inspired by the Holy Spirit! So, when you read from the Bible and think about what you're reading, you're actually doing a form of prayer. It's actually pretty simple.

Examination of Conscience

This is used a lot before going to confession, but it's also something that's great to do every day! To examine your conscience, you just have to think about all of the things that you have done that may not make God very happy. If you are having trouble of thinking of any ideas, a good place to start would be to take a look at the Ten Commandments.

- Have you lied recently?
- Have you done everything that your parents have asked you to do?
- Have you fought with your siblings or friends?
- Have you been envious (jealous) of a friend's new iPod or phone or vacation?

This is a good place to start, but there are always more examples of things that you could have done that might not make God happy. When you do an Examination of Conscience, ask God to help you fix the problems that you have been having in your life. And don't give up on yourself or think that you are too terrible of a person to continue praying. Remember that God loves you! No matter what you have done, He will *always* love you. If you talk to Him about the struggles that you have, then He can help you out with them.

Our Own Prayers

Don't forget that you can make up your own prayers, too. You and God have a relationship, and He wants to hear *your* voice. He wants to know all about your day. He wants to hear about the awful fight that you got into with your best friend. He wants to know about how proud you are of yourself for finishing your awesome science fair project. He wants to know everything! So it is always a great idea to pray to God in our own words. He loves it when you do.

Just remember: God loves you and wants to have a healthy relationship with you. And you can only have a healthy relationship with someone if you talk to them. So prayer is super, super important! Even if you only pray for about five or ten minutes every day, God will appreciate the fact that you took some time aside just for Him. Do you see why St. Therese of Lisieux was so excited to join the Carmelite Convent? She knew how important having a great relationship with God was, and she couldn't wait to get to know Him better! And if you pray every day—even if it's just for about five minutes—then you can get to know God better, too!

A Day in the Life of Sophia...

Sophia awoke to the sound of her grandmother dropping a plate in the kitchen—the loud initial crash of the plate, and then the delicate tinkling sound of the glass as it hit the floor. She rolled over and glanced blearily at her clock. It was seven o'clock, fifteen minutes before she had to get up for school. She groaned and pulled her covers over her head. But her grandmother had other plans for her.

"Sophia!" her grandmother called from the kitchen. "Please come down here and help me take care of this mess."

Sophia sighed. She was so tired, and she didn't want to help her grandmother pick up the broken pieces of the plate. She wanted to stay right where she was, all snug and warm in bed, the big, thick quilt pulled up over the top of her head. But she remembered that her grandmother was old, old and frail, and that her mother always told her that helping her grandmother was the least she could do. Sophia sighed and rolled out of bed, her toes curling as they hit the chilly wooden floorboards of her bedroom floor.

She hurried towards her door, stopping when she realized that the note that she had posted on the door a week ago for herself was still there. It read: "Don't forget to pray!" She had almost forgotten to pray! She had been trying to pray every morning when she woke up and every night before she went to bed because Mrs. Riley, her Sunday school teacher, had told her that it would be a good idea to pray a lot during Lent. Sophia knelt down by the edge of her bed to pray.

She prayed about the first things that came into her head, "Dear God, thank you for today. Please let it be a good day. Thank you for my friends, especially Emma, since she's been sick. And please, God, let me be good at basketball in gym today."

"Sophia Marie!" Her grandmother's sharp, warning tone cut through Sophia's thoughts.

Sophia rapidly muttered the final words of her prayer, "And please God, let me help grandma and not be grumpy about it. Amen."

She hurried downstairs to see her grandmother holding a broom in one hand and a dustpan in the other.

"There you are!" Her grandmother said. "Can you help me clean up this mess? Be careful with the glass and make sure not to cut yourself."

Sophia mustered a smile and nodded, "Of course, grandma."

By the time that Sophia arrived at school about an hour later, she already knew that this was going to be a bad day. Cleaning up the glass actually ended up taking a lot longer than her grandmother or she had expected, and by the time that she was finished, she hadn't had time to eat breakfast and she'd been forced to run to catch the bus. Emma was apparently still sick with a cold, and Sophia had been forced to sit alone. She had spent the majority of the bus ride staring out the window, watching the mixture of snow and ice melt against the window and slide down the pane. A quiet voice in her mind had whispered to God, "Why do I have to sit alone? Can't you please, please let Emma come in later today and sit next to me on the ride home?"

The first three hours of school went by normally. Sophia was just finishing up her social studies worksheet when the bell rang for lunch. There was a mad rush to be first in line at the door. Sophia ended up squished between Janie Collins and Madison Rivers. Janie and Madison were best friends. Sophia had known them both since kindergarten and they never seemed to be apart from each other. Janie was short and brown-eyed, with a sleek blonde ponytail that bounced up and down whenever she talked. Madison, on the other hand, was tall and thin, with long black hair that she wore in a braid. The two girls wore matching friendship bracelets and had half-heart lockets that matched up and formed a whole heart. Sophia knew, because Janie had shown her hers one day on the playground.

"See," she had said, pulling her half of the locket out from underneath her tank top. "My half says 'best,' and Maddie's half says, 'friends.' We made a deal to never ever take them off no matter how long we live. I'm going to live to be at least a hundred, so I'll be wearing my half for at least ninety years!"

Sophia had felt left out, but she had nodded and smiled. She had decided that maybe she and Emma could get friendship lockets the next time they went to the store with Emma's mom. Janie had been more than happy to show off her heart locket to Sophia on that afternoon on the playground, but right now she wasn't looking so happy. In fact, she was glaring at Sophia, her thin arms crossed in disapproval.

"You can't stand there," Janie said. "That's Maddie's place. Maddie and I always stand next to each other in the lunch line." Her ponytail still bounced, but it was an angry sort of bounce.

"But I got here before Maddie," Sophia protested. She didn't really see how it mattered who Janie was standing next to in line. The line only lasted for ten minutes, anyway.

Madison crossed her arms, too. "So what? We're still best friends, and best friends stand next to each other in line. You aren't our friend."

Madison's words hit Sophia like a slap. She felt the anger and the hurt that they provoked churning in her stomach. She wanted to tell

Madison that she was right—that they weren't friends, and that she was glad of it, too.

Janie nodded emphatically, her ponytail jerking up and down. "Yeah, Sophia! Madison, come up here with me." She stared at Sophia, her brown eyes narrowing. "And if you tell on us, we'll tell Miss Willet that you tripped Maddie on the bus today and that you're just making things up to get us in trouble."

Sophia opened her mouth to tell Janie and Madison exactly what she thought of them, but at the last second, she remembered what her grandmother always told her—that it was better to say nothing at all than to say something mean. So instead of yelling at them, she simply bit her lip and talked to God instead. "God, Madison and Janie make me so mad! They're being so mean to me, and I didn't even do anything to them. I know I'm supposed to be nice to everyone, but it is really hard. Can you please help me?"

Madison slipped past Sophia, casting Sophia a triumphant look. She and Janie immediately put their heads together and began to whisper and giggle. Every once in a while, they looked back at Sophia and smirked.

It made Sophia feel sick to her stomach. But she knew that she was doing the right thing, with God's help. Her grandmother would be so proud of her!

Miss Willet came hurrying up to the front of the line, "Okay, everybody, we're ready to head down to lunch. Remember to be quiet in the halls!"

The rest of the day was pretty uneventful, but Sophia felt her stomach clench with dread when the last bell rang. It was time to go home on the bus, but God hadn't answered her prayer about Emma coming back to school. Why wouldn't God answer her prayers? Her grandmother had always told her that God always answered prayers. Sophia's fear about sitting on the bus all alone was made even worse by her realization that Madison and Janie would be there, too. They would probably sit behind her and whisper and giggle together about how she didn't have anyone to sit with.

As she climbed the stairs on the bus with a heavy heart, Sophia asked God, "Why couldn't you answer my prayer? I just wanted Emma to get better so she could sit on the bus with me. And now Madison and Janie are going to make fun of me for sitting alone!"

As she sat down in her seat, her heart sank even further. Here came Madison and Janie already, whispering on the sidewalk, their bright red backpacks a perfect match. As they climbed the bus stairs, Sophia stared out of her window, hoping that they would ignore her. Her thoughts were interrupted, however, by the sound of an unfamiliar girl's voice.

"Hey, is it okay if I sit here?" the girl asked.

Sophia turned to see who it was that was talking to her. A girl she had never seen before—red-haired, plump, and freckled—was smiling at her. Her bright blue eyes seemed friendly from behind her silver glasses.

Sophia smiled back. "Sure!"

She patted the seat next to her.

The red-haired girl sat down. "Thank you! I'm Ellie. I just moved here, so I don't know anyone yet. What's your name?"

"I'm Sophia," Sophia said. "Where are you from?"

"I'm from California," Ellie said.

"That's so cool! Where in California are you from?" Sophia asked.

The two girls spent the rest of the bus ride talking to each other. Sophia found out that Ellie loved sledding just as much as she did, and the two girls planned to go to Hazel Hill sometime together with Ellie's parents. Ellie promised to show Sophia her collection of horseback riding posters, and Sophia promised to show Ellie her collection of signed basketball posters.

Even Madison and Janie seemed interested in Ellie. They were too busy listening to her stories about California to whisper and giggle like usual. Just as Sophia was about to get off at her stop, Janie stopped her by putting a hand on her arm.

"I'm sorry that Madison and I told you that you weren't our friend," Janie said. "I hope that you and Ellie can sit with Madison and me at lunch tomorrow."

Madison smiled and nodded. "I hope so, too."

Sophia smiled. "We'll see," she said.

The bus driver honked her horn in impatience. "I have to go," Sophia said. "Bye, Maddie. Bye, Janie. Bye, Ellie. It was so nice to meet you!"

Ellie waved good-bye to Sophia from the bus window. Sophia smiled and waved back. It was so nice to make a new friend! Maybe that was why God hadn't sent Emma back to school early. He must have known that Sophia was going to make a new friend! Maybe her grandmother was right: God did answer all prayers, but not always exactly the way that you expect 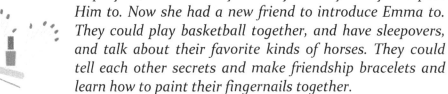 Him to. Now she had a new friend to introduce Emma to. They could play basketball together, and have sleepovers, and talk about their favorite kinds of horses. They could tell each other secrets and make friendship bracelets and learn how to paint their fingernails together.

Sophia spun around in a circle in pure delight. There were so many things to be thankful for, and so many things to look forward to!

Glossary

Catechism of the Catholic Church

The *Catechism of the Catholic Church* is the official text on what the Catholic Church teaches and believes. If you ever have a question about what the Catholic Church believes, the *Catechism* is a great place to start! If you need to, you can always ask an adult to help you understand what the *Catechism* is really saying, too.

Chastity

Chastity is a virtue (a good trait). People who are chaste are pure in their minds, their bodies, and their hearts. Their purity shows in their attitudes, behavior, and appearance. They strive to be innocent. They are modest. They do not wear super short skirts, or show a lot of skin. Girls who are chaste also do not chase after boys or talk about boys all the time to their friends.

Communion of Saints

When you say the Apostles' Creed, the last couple of lines that you say are: "I believe in the Holy Spirit, the holy Catholic Church, the communion of saints, the forgiveness of sins, the resurrection of the body, and life everlasting. Amen." So, what exactly are the communion of saints? The communion of saints refers to the faithful people on earth, the souls in purgatory (the place where souls go if they need to be cleaned up a little bit before going to Heaven), and the souls in Heaven. All of these souls are bound together in one body. Christ is the head of this body.

Debt

This is when you owe somebody something. A lot of times it means that you owe money to another person. If you have borrowed $10 from your friend, for instance, you owe them that money back. You usually don't want to be in debt, but if you know that you will have money later to pay that person back, then it is okay. People also go into debt a lot of the time when they are buying big things, like a house. As long as you have a plan for paying off your debt, there's no need for concern!

Easter Vigil

The Easter Vigil is a very special Mass that takes place on the evening of Holy Saturday, in the darkness before the dawn of Easter Sunday morning. It is usually about three hours long, and it celebrates Jesus' rising from the dead. Maybe you have noticed that during Lent, nobody says the word, "Alleluia," and nobody sings the *Gloria* at Mass. The Easter Vigil is the first Mass after Lent in which people sing the *Gloria* and say the word, "Alleluia!"

Eucharistic Adoration

Eucharistic Adoration is a very special kind of prayer. You know that a consecrated host has actually become Jesus, right? Well, in Eucharistic Adoration, the consecrated host (also known as the Blessed Sacrament) is displayed so that people can pray with Jesus right there in the same room! The Blessed Sacrament is held in a very special vessel (container) called a monstrance.

Examination of Conscience

An examination of conscience is something that you should try to do every day! It is really pretty simple. At the end of the day, as you think about all of the things that you've done, try to think about any sins you may have committed, and ask God for forgiveness for those sins. Ask Him for the strength to stop committing those sins in the future, too! *Here is a cool way to do an examination of conscience:* Start by imagining yourself near to God. Then, think of all the good things that have happened to you throughout the day. These were gifts from God! Next, think about all of the ways that you have fallen short throughout the day. Did you sin at all? Ask for God's forgiveness! Lastly, thank God for the gifts that He gave you throughout the day, and ask Him to help you with the things that you struggle with.

Feminine Genius

This is the term that Pope John Paul II (see glossary entry for more) gave to describe the gifts that God gave especially to girls. The words also describe the special kind of intelligence that girls have!

Final Resurrection

One of the amazing promises that Jesus made to His followers was that He would raise the bodies of the dead to Heaven. So, what exactly does this mean? First of all, you are made of two distinct things: your soul and your body. Your soul is the most important part of you, and can't be seen or touched. It's something inside of you. Your body is your physical self. On earth, God combines your soul and your body to create – well, you! Together, the soul and the body make you into who you are! When people die, as long as they are in a state of grace, their souls will go to Heaven. But their bodies won't go with them to Heaven until the Judgment Day. The Judgment Day is the day that Jesus will judge the souls of the men and women still living on earth. It is the last day that earth will exist. Nobody knows when the Judgment Day will come, but we do know – from Jesus' promise to us – that when it does come, He will restore people's bodies to them. <u>Learn More!</u> Read more about this in the Bible (1 Cor. 15:35–44, 1 John 3:2), and in the *Catechism of the Catholic Church* (CCC 988-1019).

Forgiveness of Sins
One of the most important things that Jesus taught us about in the Bible is forgiveness. He said that it is extremely important to forgive others, especially people who have hurt us. Think about it! Even though Jesus was perfect and without sin, He forgave the people who scourged (whipped) Him and crucified Him. If Jesus can forgive people for doing such horrible things, you can forgive people for hurting you, too!

Genuflection
When you genuflect, you bend at least one knee to the ground. Genuflection shows respect, so always make sure to genuflect towards the tabernacle (a special container for the Blessed Sacrament) when you are entering and leaving church. It's a way of showing that you respect Jesus!

God the Father
God the Father is the creator of the world. He is eternal, and exists outside of time. That means that He doesn't notice time the same way that you do! He is also all-knowing and all-powerful. He created each and every one of us out of pure love. He wants you to love Him, too! God the Father loved us so much that He sent His only Son, Jesus Christ, to die for our sins. That's pretty amazing. God is also part of the Trinity, along with Jesus Christ and the Holy Spirit.

Grace
Grace is a gift that God gives us freely because He loves us. The goal of grace is to help us get to Heaven. You have probably experienced grace before! Here are some examples of ways that people can experience grace:
- ❖ Hearing a song that makes them remember to be thankful for everything that God has given them.
- ❖ Waking up in the morning and wanting to pray because it is a beautiful day!

These are examples of grace because they are invitations from God to get closer to Him. If you take these opportunities to get closer to God, it will strengthen your relationship with Him!

Handmaid of the Lord
A handmaid is female servant or attendant. The Virgin Mary (see the glossary entry for more) is often described as the "handmaid of the lord." This description is a compliment! Mary was so special that she was chosen to attend to (to serve), God and the Messiah. The perfect handmaid would be obedient and happy to serve. Mary truly is an example of the perfect handmaid, then, because she made the choice to follow God's will!

Holy Catholic Church
If you are reading this book, you are probably part of the Holy Catholic Church. This is an amazing privilege to have! The Catholic Church was founded by *Jesus Christ* (see the glossary entry for more info!). The Catholic Church bases its beliefs on two different things – the Bible, which is the inspired word of God, and Holy Tradition. What is Holy Tradition? The *Catechism of the Catholic Church* describes it this way: "[Holy] Tradition transmits in its entirety the Word of God which has been entrusted to the apostles by Christ the Lord and the Holy Spirit" (CCC 81). That may seem kind of hard to understand. Basically, Jesus trusted His Apostles to pass down His teachings throughout the ages. Holy Tradition, then, are the teachings that the Apostles and their successors (the people that came after them) passed down. The successors of the Apostles are the bishops of the Catholic Church. Pretty cool, huh?

Holy Spirit
The Holy Spirit is the third part of the Trinity. The Holy Spirit gives us both *grace* (see the glossary entry!) and spiritual gifts and fruits. There are seven gifts of the Holy Spirit. They are: the gift of wisdom, the gift of understanding, the gift of counsel, the gift of fortitude (mental and emotional strength), the gift of knowledge, the gift of piety (having respect or reverence for God), and the gift of fear (which helps us to respect God's great power).

Jesus Christ
Jesus Christ is the Son of God, the Messiah, and Savior of the world. God sent Jesus, His only Son, to save the world through His death and His resurrection (rising up from the dead). Jesus spent his life teaching about his Father and the good news of salvation (that people could be washed clean of their sins and go to Heaven). He gathered many Apostles and followers throughout his lifetime. He also performed many miracles, curing the sick, opening the eyes of the blind, and even raising men from the dead. His greatest miracle of all, however, was to die on the cross for us, and to rise again, three days later. By willingly dying on the cross for us, Jesus gave each and every one of us the chance for eternal (never-ending) life in Heaven. Jesus is both fully divine and fully human, and is part of the Trinity.

Life Everlasting
One of the things that Jesus promised us in the Bible was life everlasting. That means that the souls of people who have been faithful to God and to Jesus will go to Heaven, where they will love and praise God forever!

Mass

Whenever you go to church on Sunday, you are going to Mass. There are two main parts of the Mass: the Liturgy of the Word and the Liturgy of the Eucharist. There are also rites (a ceremonial act) at the beginning and end of Mass. The readings, the homily (sermon), the Profession of Faith (when you say the Nicene Creed), and the Prayer of the Faithful are all part of the Liturgy of the Word. The Liturgy of the Eucharist includes the consecration (making the bread and wine into the body and the blood), and Communion.

Pope John Paul II

Pope John Paul II was born with the name Karol Józef Wojtyla. He changed his name to John Paul II when he was elected Pope in October of 1978. He was Pope for over 25 years! Pope John Paul II was one of the most influential leaders in the 20th century. He died on April 2, 2005. He was beatified in 2011. That means that he's on the way to becoming declared a saint! Right now, he is known as "Blessed."

Pope Benedict XVI

Pope Benedict XVI is the 266th pope in succession from the time of Peter. He was elected pope on April 19, 2005.

Pro-Life

People who are pro-life see the worth and dignity of every person, even of babies still in the mother's womb. They care about babies, and believe that it is very wrong for a woman to have an abortion. When a woman has an abortion, she allows a "doctor" to kill the baby in her womb. People who are pro-life understand that this is murder – taking away an innocent life – and that it is also usually harmful to the woman getting the abortion. They want to stop this horrible practice.

Rosary

The rosary is a special form of prayer that helps you meditate on (think about) Jesus' life. It also helps show devotion to the Virgin Mary, Jesus' mother! A rosary is generally made with beads (or knotted string), which help you keep track of how many prayers you have said. The prayer that is said the most often while praying the rosary is the "Hail, Mary." To help you meditate upon the life of Jesus there are different "mysteries" that can be said. Each set of mysteries is focused on a certain thing. The mysteries are: Luminous, Joyful, Sorrowful, and Glorious.

Sacraments

A sacrament is an outward sign of the grace that God gives each and every one of us. By participating in sacraments, you actually receive grace, as well! If you don't know what *grace* is, go ahead and take a look at the glossary entry for it!
How Many Are There? What Are They? There are seven sacraments. They are: Baptism, Confirmation, the Holy Eucharist (also known as Communion), the Sacrament of Reconciliation (also known as Confession), Anointing of the Sick, Holy Orders, and the Sacrament of Matrimony (also known as marriage).

Sin: Venial and Mortal

The *Catechism of the Catholic Church* defines sin as "an offense against God." God created us to love and serve Him, and any time we turn away from doing these things, we are sinning. Sin is harmful to us because it separates us from God. There are less serious sins (called venial sins), and more serious sins (called mortal sins).
Venial Sins: Venial sins separate you from God, but they don't cause you to lose sight of Him completely. An example of a venial sin might be gossiping.
Mortal Sins: Mortal sins cause you to lose sight of God. In order for something to be a mortal sin, it has to:
1. Be a serious sin. This means that it has to break one of the Ten Commandments.
2. Be done with the full knowledge of the person. This means that the person has to know that what they are doing is a serious wrong.
3. Be done with the full agreement of the person. This means that the person was not forced into sinning.

Stations of the Cross

This is a special kind of prayer called a *devotion*. A person who is praying the Stations of the Cross meditates, or thinks, about all of the stages of Jesus' crucifixion, from the time He was condemned to die by Pontius Pilate to the time when He was laid in His tomb. There are often carvings or statues of each stage of the Stations of the Cross, which help the person praying think and feel more deeply about Christ's crucifixion. There are 14 Stations of the Cross.

Tithing

Did you know that the Catholic Church asks you to give away about 10 percent of everything that you make throughout the year to the church or to other charitable organizations? They do! This is a practice called tithing.

Transubstantiation

Transubstantiation is the change that the bread and wine goes through during Mass to become the Body and Blood of Jesus Christ. That is why getting the opportunity to receive the Eucharist is such an amazing experience! When you receive the Eucharist, you become one body with all the members of the Catholic Church and Christ.

Virgin Mary

The Virgin Mary was chosen by God to be Jesus Christ's mother. When the angel Gabriel appeared to her and asked her if she would be Jesus' mother, she agreed. This agreement showed her love and obedience to God. Mary was born without sin. She is the only human being (other than Jesus, who was also fully divine) to be born without sin. She also lived her entire life without sinning. That is hard to imagine, isn't it? Since Mary was the mother of Jesus, Catholics believe that Mary is a mother to all Christians! There are some very special prayers that are said in honor of the Virgin Mary, including the rosary.

Virtues: Theological and Cardinal

There are two main types of virtues: theological and cardinal.
Theological Virtues: There are three theological virtues. They are: faith (belief in God), hope (expecting and desiring to receive something), and charity (loving one's neighbor). Theological virtues are given to us through grace – in other words, they are a gift from God. They help people get to Heaven.
Cardinal Virtues: There are four cardinal virtues. They are: prudence, justice, restraint, and courage. Prudence helps you to make good decisions. Being just means balancing your own self-interest with the good of other people. Having restraint means being able to control your actions. Finally, being courageous means being able to stand up to fear. The cardinal virtues help people to live good, moral lives.

Vocation

There are a couple of different meanings of the word "vocation."
- ❖ A person's state in life. For example, if someone is going to get married, that is their vocation. Similarly, if someone is going to take their vows to become a nun or a sister, that is their vocation.
- ❖ A person's personal relationship with Jesus Christ. Your personal vocation is to love Jesus! You are given this vocation at baptism, when you become a Christian.

Womb

The womb is a special place in a woman's body where babies grow. The technical word for a womb is "uterus." Babies usually spend about nine months in the mother's womb. The mother carries the baby inside of her womb so that it can grow healthy and strong. Because the mother carries the baby inside her own body, there is a special connection between the two of them. Biblical Connections: There are lots of mothers who carried babies in their wombs in the Old and New Testament. Maybe the one that you are most familiar with is Mary, the mother of Jesus. She carried Jesus safely in her womb until He was born in the manger at Bethlehem.

Answer Key for page 60: 1 is Henriette Delille; 2 is St. Genevieve; 3 is Margaret Clitherow; 4 is St. Lydia; 5 is St. Elizabeth of Portugal; 6 is St. Juliana of Liege

Answer Key for page 48 Manners Quiz: The Politeness Princess ~ If you mostly answered "almost always," then you are a Politeness Princess. Congratulations! You go beyond the basics of being polite. You always try to think of others before yourself, and you try not to say things that will upset people, unless if you think that it is absolutely necessary for their own good. Great job! Keep it up! Pretty Polite ~ If you mostly answered "sometimes," then you are pretty polite. You have the basics of being polite down, but you may sometimes forget to send the occasional "thank-you" card. You're doing pretty well overall, though! Polish Your Politeness ~ If you mostly answered "never," then you might need to work on polishing your politeness. It's okay, though, because everything comes with practice! If you practice saying "thank you," and "I'm sorry," enough, you'll soon find that being polite comes naturally!

CPSIA information can be obtained at www.ICGtesting.com
Printed in the USA
BVOW10s1226101113

335920BV00001B/1/P